We Made a PACT

Promise of Accountability,
Commitment and Trust

by
Chris and Carol Green

Unless otherwise noted, all scripture quotations are from the New King James Version of the Bible.

We Made a PACT:
Promise of Accountability, Commitment and Trust

ISBN-13: 978-1463605308
ISBN-10: 1463605307

Published by: Fruitful Life Network, Incorporated

Cover Design: CreateSpace.com

Photography: Amethyst Roberson

Edited by: Carol L. Green

Printed in the United States of America

For more information on other publications and products contact:

Chris and Carol Green

Fruitful Life Network, Incorporated
http://www.fruitful-life.net

Table of Contents

Dedications   5

Prologue   7

Introduction   11

Our Story   15

Promise   29

Accountability   47

Commitment   73

Trust   85

Climate Change   97

Acknowledgements   101

Bibliography and References   102

About the Authors   103

Dedications

To James and Jane Green, who married January 10, 1954, and stayed together in spite of incredible pain, heartaches and heartbreak.

Even though family tragedy, overwhelming losses and inexplicable calamity were part of the fabric of your lives, you still managed to impart a desire to do the best with what we have been given and to live for something greater than ourselves. You passed these values on to your children, grandchildren and great grandchildren.

You were the perfect choice by God, to be an example for us to learn from and follow.

To the best man, Jonathan Green, and maid of honor,
Janeth Harrison ...we will never forget.

Prologue

Since I first met Chris and Carol Green, I've marveled at how their ministry displays the epitome of "team players". In my estimation, their relationship is a testament of how, if we let God deal with the mess in us in private, when the world sees us, we can be polished and refined like a tree that bears big beautiful fruit. I can see the fruit of "We Made a Pact" manifesting in people's lives in many ways. One of them being, the knowledge that the "pact" that we make with one another must be sealed with an agreement that no matter what, in the end God wins in every area of our lives. The other being the impact we will have on each other's lives when we realize that no one is perfect except the One who sits on the Throne.

Once we humble ourselves before Him, He uses our lives to impact others "even while we are sleeping". I believe that just as you can identify a tree by its fruit, so you can identify people by their actions. A good tree cannot produce bad fruit, and a bad tree cannot produce good fruit says the Word of God. Myself, I have chosen to trust God and be a person of integrity who is deemed to be trustworthy. This is what you will also learn about Chris and Carol Green as you read their lives through this book.

When I read the chapter on "Trust", I immediately thought of how important it is to trust the person with whom you are in covenant, whether it is business-related or personal. I happen to focus in on the business side of relationships since I have owned a production company since the age of nineteen. Being a producer has caused me to encounter some major "trust related" setbacks with many different individuals.

Producers produce jobs, which in turn, establish many contractual relationships that require trust from all parties involved. If that pact is breached in any way, all involved suffer. So in life, when you are committed to someone, just as in a marriage, the pact should be unbreakable.

I am reminded of the time that I received the phone call from my good friend James "JT" Thomas. "JT" helped me to seal my biggest deal yet, in Hollywood, with comedian Steve Harvey to produce my stage play, "A Woman's Worth". I could hear in his voice how excited he was for me; even though I couldn't even express my excitement because of the shock that it all happened so fast. We met at Roscoe's Chicken and Waffles one sunny afternoon in L.A. so he could find out what I needed to make the show happen. In just a few weeks the deal was done!

I must admit, I had been promised a lot of things from a lot of people in California that never came to pass. So I had to put my total trust in God's promise to me and then wait for everything to happen just as He said it would. For it is one thing for someone to say they are going to do something for you and another when they actually do it. Things escalate to a whole new level when that person commits to seeing it through to the end.

Just like Chris and Carol, I believe that's exactly why keeping your word is so important in everything that you do. Most people want to know that you are "down for them" when the storm comes, not just when the sun is shining. It helps to build a solid foundation in a relationship that cannot be shaken or moved by any outside source. That's why I was so touched by the words Chris stated to Carol after a disagreement they had with one another. That's a true bond that has the God-kind of staying power that He can and does use mightily through them in this book.

Trust should be a major factor in any relationship and personally without it, I will not move an inch. My business partners have to trust that I am on the same page with them at every turn because in this business, if you show any sign of dissention within the camp, you put everyone relying on you in jeopardy.

To those who love to read about relationships, this book will be a page-turner. However, for those who like to apply what they read, the highlighter and notepad will be required. Chris and Carol Green have written a jewel, with remarkable transparency, to those who desire to establish great, Godly relationships with the depth and complexity needed to last forever.

I received a powerful word from Chris and Carol Green regarding our company and the blessings God had in store for us. I was honored to write a prologue for the life changing book they have written called, "We Made a Pact".

Chrys Yvette, Playwright/Producer/Director/Actress
Chrys Yvette Productions

Introduction

We found ourselves celebrating our 30th wedding anniversary with sober reflection. We did not have the festive feelings of the previous years. There was mainly a strong desire to put our story in writing so that our children and grandchildren would know about their legacy of love.

Our 20th anniversary celebration had been very exciting. It included a vow renewal ceremony, purchasing our first real wedding ring, a wonderful celebration with family and friends, and the release of several songs on a CD to commemorate the occasion. The 25th anniversary came and went with very little fanfare because we were deeply involved in our new ministry in Pennsylvania.

However, the 30th anniversary was spent taking a long drive, a late night of dining, and sharing countless memories. That trip down memory lane reminded us that we had never really told our story or focused on marriage in our ministry in Pennsylvania. We had only taught about it in our home church's pre-marital classes, and in seminars and workshops as part of itinerant travels.

Behind the scenes we had advised scores of couples that were contemplating marriage or divorce. We didn't have piles of data, charts, diagrams and official analysis based upon years of research to back up what we offered a couple. All we had was life's experience and the Bible, yet we were bold and forthright.

Once we became the senior leaders of a faith family in south central Pennsylvania, we were faced with an endless list of matters that needed to be addressed. However, marriage was the one topic that we did not tackle head on because it was a very sensitive issue in this region.

The city, in which our ministry was planted, had a long history of marriages breaking apart. It was devastated by broken marriages, relationships and homes. Carol had firsthand experience with this reality because she was returning to her hometown, where her mom and dad separated when she was 12 years old. They never got back together and eventually divorced. It was no surprise that the majority of the first attendees to our church were either divorced or the product of divorce. For some, their parents had never married.

There was so much more that needed to be dealt with beyond the topic of marriage, that it wasn't until the fourth year of our Pennsylvania ministry that we could begin to address relationship topics in any consistent teaching series. Even then, the approach was to initiate discussions with young adults in the context of pre-marital preparation.

After our 30th anniversary celebration, we felt it was time to focus on families for the first time in the ministry. It was time to launch a strategic set of teachings that would begin to rebuild, restore and renew hearts and homes in our small community of Believers.

When the New Year of 2011 rolled in, the first time our church family gathered was on the second Sunday in the month of January. That was the day we began to strategically teach about the PACT we made as six-month-old newlyweds.

Through the years, and throughout all of the many public sessions and personal advice, we almost always referred to this one decision in our marriage, as the single most important one that we ever made. It was when we made that special promise. So we named our teaching series accordingly, **The PACT**.

In previous years we also held back on writing a relationship book because there are so many others, in our opinion, who are better qualified to teach about marriage and family; others who have the expertise and credentials to do so.

It has never been our intent to minimize or belittle the benefits of educational training and preparation to enhance one's ability to guide individuals and couples through the challenges of the marriage relationship.

That's why this book makes no attempt to deceive the reader in to thinking these words are coming only from Chris and Carol Green. In fact, throughout this book we will refer to specialists who have the training and qualifications. Some of them are the same professionals who helped us in critical seasons of our marriage.

This book is not a marriage 'how to' instructional. It is a 'life-principles' manual in which wisdom and understanding can be gleaned from the pages as you relive the journey of two lowly inner city kids who dropped out of college, made lots of mistakes, and came together in holy matrimony. We also wanted to set the record straight regarding our premarital failures. We wanted to tell our story and give God the Glory.

When we reached that first moment of marital impasse, we made a simple promise to one another. Now after more than thirty years, we are sharing the results of that promise and the priceless treasure that we have acquired.

Our Story

We were married at a Justice of the Peace office in downtown Tulsa, Oklahoma on December 29, 1980. However, an official wedding ceremony still awaited us, five days later, on January 3, 1981. Our original plan was to only go to the JP, but my family (especially my brother Mark Green) insisted on providing a wedding and reception for us in St. Louis, Missouri, so we reluctantly agreed. When we look at our wedding photos today, we're very thankful that we agreed.

The laws state that you must get married within the same state in which you obtain your marriage license. We couldn't get a license in Oklahoma and then get married in Missouri. So, we had to get married in Oklahoma, before our ceremony. That's how we came to be standing before a Justice of the Peace.

Right from the beginning, we found ourselves getting married twice to start our journey as husband and wife. And to answer that one question that most will ask; yes, we still waited until after the church wedding ceremony.

We first met in August of 1977 on the campus of Oral Roberts University. I was sitting in Mabee Center, where they play the basketball games. It was a huge place and students were dispersed throughout the arena according to whatever major in which they were enrolling. I was completing my paperwork when I noticed a nice looking Black girl sitting about three rows behind me and on the far end of the section. She had a reddish complexion, reddish hair, was very slender and wore a white dress. My first thought was "O, another Black person."
I didn't give her a second look because I didn't want to start that awkward –oops I got caught staring routine.

Carol recalls: *I was sitting in Mabee Center, looking around and listening to the orientation speech. I was very nervous and looking for a friend whom I knew should be in the same meeting. In the sea of White faces I began looking for Black faces to help me not to feel so out of place.*

Then I saw a Black young man sitting in the same section in the rows below me. It helped me not to feel so alien and he had a little smirk on his face. It made me wonder what he was thinking. A wayward thought drifted across my mind, "I wonder if he's my husband". I immediately canceled it, particularly since that kind of thinking was a "fad" at that time and one I didn't want to emulate.

***

After the orientation session, the students were dismissed and we were allowed to continue walking around the campus to get familiar with our new environment.

As hundreds of students walked across the campus, I saw a childhood friend that I had not seen since our eighth grade graduation. It was quite a surprise to see her, now four years later. Her name was Wilma Calvert. She was walking with that same girl I'd seen earlier in the Mabee Center. I greeted Wilma with warmth and delight. Then she turned and introduced me to that girl.

At that time in my life, I was extremely melancholy. I was born into a grief stricken family because my mother was seven months pregnant with me when her youngest child died in a horrible food choking accident. Many professionals believe that an unborn baby is directly impacted by the emotional state of its mother. Paralyzing grief, deep depression and pervasive pessimism was embedded in my soul. As I grew up, most of the time, I was the saddest toddler, adolescent and teenager you could have possibly encountered.

Also, while growing up in inner city St. Louis, Missouri, I had a few experiences that led me to become very cold when meeting a young lady. It was a self-taught response, but there was a lot of pain behind it.

One day I passed by two girls as I was leaving the high school building. I overheard one girl say to the other as she looked at me, "This school sho' aint got no nice lookin' niggas."

So, of course my self-esteem was crushed in the moment.

I didn't think I was all that great looking anyway, but a comment like that sure didn't help much. Even before those words were spoken, I was already a critical mass of self-loathing and self-hatred.

Basically, I trained myself to be polite, but show no interest, one way or the other. So, as I looked at this new girl who was being introduced to me, I nodded my head and almost whispered, "Hi."

This girl didn't like my response and she blurted,

"Well, aren't you going to speak?"

I thought I had just done that. I mustered up a little more effort and said it a little louder, "Hi."

Carol recalls: *A dorm friend I just met from St. Louis suggested we go to lunch together at the cafeteria. As we were on the way she met a friend from her hometown, and to my surprise it was that young man. They greeted each other and talked a little bit when Wilma introduced us to one another. I said hi and he just sorta, kinda nodded his head. For some reason this irritated me.*

"Well," I said, "Aren't you going to speak?

I was just as surprised as he was, by the expression on his face. He said hi. Wilma, watching this interchange, decided to play matchmaker. She suggested that we all go to lunch together.

***

It was not the kind of start that would lead anyone to believe we were destined to get married someday.

A couple of days later, we were in the same lecture hall. Unknown to one another, we were enrolled in three courses together. This was one of them. After the class, as students poured out of the room, several other Black students and I were floating in the area. One of my new friends (Mark Lawrence) introduced me to that same girl I had met during orientation. This time my response was friendlier and this time I remembered her name, Carol Dennis.

Yes, it took being introduced twice to get us to talk to one another. Maybe that's why it took getting married twice to get that to stick, too.

Our relationship was very slow to develop. However, Wilma was very good at helping us to move things along. She would invite us to lunch, and then slip away, leaving the two of us to talk.

We found that we had a lot in common, especially writing. We agreed to swap our personal notebooks that were filled with poems. Then we agreed to meet in the Prayer Gardens to talk about our writings. Carol took the opportunity to slip in a poem about me.

After reading that poem, I knew that I needed to nip this obvious attraction, in the bud. I had a girlfriend back home in St. Louis. I needed to tell Carol the truth up front.

We met one balmy summer evening in the beautiful gardens that were situated directly beneath ORU's prayer tower. It was a beautiful summer evening. The stars were bright. The breeze was perfect. The setting was complete with the golden glow of the garden lanterns.

First we talked about the notebooks. I asked her about that certain poem as I pretended that I didn't know whom she was talking about. I inquired if it was about an old boyfriend back in Pennsylvania. She never answered me directly.

During the conversation, Carol expressed how she was tired of boys who play around with your feelings. In one of her poems she had written her ultimatum of people accepting her as she was or leaving her alone. I used that poem to set up what I needed to say. I told her that I didn't want to lead her on because I had a girlfriend back home. I told her we could just be friends.

Carol recalls: *I enjoyed the conversations I had with Chris because he is very intelligent and quick witted. I was pleasantly surprised that I could have an intelligent conversation with someone my own age.*

Most young men seemed to either feel intimidated or weren't interested in talking, so to find a young man who was attractive, intelligent, taller than me and loved God; it was too much!

We were to meet in the Prayer Garden to talk about our writings, so I thought I would slip in a poem about Chris that just seemed to write itself. I wanted to see his response. We were friends, but I wanted to see if he would give more. At the very least I wanted to know where he was concerning our growing relationship.

When we met, that perfect summer evening, he told me about his girlfriend, that he didn't want to lead me on, and that we could continue to be friends. I decided to be the best friend he ever had; especially since he confided that his relationship with his girlfriend was what we call a 'church' relationship, meaning most of the time they spent together was at church and conversation on the telephone.

***

Throughout the remainder of the semester, we tried to just be friends, but we had three classes together, twice a week. We ate together. We studied together. It was obvious that we had something special.

When I walked her to her dormitory, I gave her the brotherly hug, no lingering and no extra squeeze. I just didn't want to be messing with her feelings. I was also trying to honor my commitment back home.

During Thanksgiving, a defining moment came. The school was closed due to the holiday and during that weekend college students are left to fend for themselves. This was our first Thanksgiving away from home and a friend of a friend invited us to their home for Thanksgiving dinner.

As soon as we walked up to the door of the friend's house, I rang the doorbell, turned around to Carol and said, "I love you." Then I gasped in total shock that those words had come out of my mouth. I said it without thinking and they flowed out as easily as a breath.

However, at that moment I was trying to suck the words back into my mouth. Carol's eyebrows raised as her eyes brightened. I could almost hear her say, "I knew it!"

I tried to play it off and say that I love this time of the year or something like that, but it was too late. My true feelings had spilled out. Afterwards, I continued to play down that incident. I never spoke of it and acted like it never happened.

Carol recalls: *That momentous Thanksgiving Day! I was just glad to have somewhere to eat real food, not cafeteria food. I was hoping we would have a good time.*

We were standing at the front of our friend's home and Chris rang the doorbell. When he turned to me and said, "I love you" and sucked in a breath as if he couldn't believe what he said, I smiled and screamed in my head, "I can't believe he said it".

I felt completely victorious. I knew that I couldn't over react or he would bolt, so I just looked at him and smiled. Then our friend opened the door to let us in.

***

When our first Christmas break came, I learned that things were dramatically different when I got back home to St. Louis. My friends and I were going through the normal process that occurs in this time of life. You go away and friends start growing away from one another. We were still just teenagers and we didn't understand what was happening to us.

My girlfriend and I didn't have much in common anymore and neither did my buddies. All the conversations were forced and awkward. We had changed a lot in just four short months. I didn't know how to handle it. I felt like some resentment started building to divide us, but that was only because none of us knew how to deal with this transition into adulthood. I couldn't wait to get back to school with all my new friends and my special relationship with Carol.

Carol recalls her Christmas break:
I was home and missing Chris. We didn't have long distance phone service on our home phone so he would call me at a neighbor's (Mom's best friend) house two doors down from where I lived. When he called I would tear out of the house to go talk to him.

I couldn't wait to go back to school. I not only missed Chris, but I missed the friends I had made who loved God like I did, and really wanted to live for God.

***

When we got back to school after Christmas break, my roommate received some Red Lobster coupons that included some free dinners. He shared some of them with me, so I asked Carol out to dinner. It was to be our first official date.

We were so nervous it was unbelievable. After all the time we had spent together, talking freely and easily, the minute we called it a date, all the dynamics changed immediately.

I tried to be a gentleman and recall every lesson on manners that I had ever been taught. I held the car door. I pulled out her chair at the table. We even prayed over the food in public. The dinner was good and the time together was nice. We survived our first date. As usual, I walked her back to her dormitory and still kept it friendly with a brotherly hug.

Carol recalls the first date: *Chris' roommate, Steve, was given coupons for Red Lobster and invited Chris and I to go out with him and his girlfriend, Becky. Chris asked if I would like to go and of course I said yes, but I was nervous about eating in front of him. I wore a favorite black three-piece pinstriped pants suit that I had made. When he opened the doors for me and pulled out my chair to seat me, it was the first time any young man had shown me such courtesy. We really enjoyed our time together. He walked me to my dorm,* *gave me the sister hug, opened the door for me and said good night.*

***

Well, our fairy tale started falling apart a couple months after that. Carol didn't have enough funds to complete the school year and was unable to attend classes.

A few of our friends tried to make an appeal directly to President Oral Roberts, but he steered them back to the financial aid office and all of the protocols that were already in place.

I noticed that Carol was completely apprehensive about the whole matter and was ready to give up without a fight. I didn't understand, at that time, why she was responding to the situation this way. It was one of those things that you observe about a person that has no meaning until after you are married to them.

Finally, the school arranged for a one-way plane ticket to send her home and we were just crushed. Everyone who knew her and knew the situation just felt so badly for her, but there was nothing that any of us could do.

The night before her morning flight, we went out to eat. I borrowed my brother's car. Once we got back to the campus, we sat in the parking lot a long, long time.

After all the time we had spent together and all that we shared in common, I just could not see a future without her in it. So I opened up and told her my true feelings. I confessed that I loved her and vowed that someday, some way, we were going to be together.

Then I kissed her. Yeah, the kiss like in the movies, with the orchestra dramatically drowning out every other sound to capture the moment. It was a kiss with tears streaming and deep sobbing that stained our hearts and permanently imprinted our vow.

Of, course when you're 18 years old and as broke as a ghetto screen door, you have no idea how you're going to make anything happen, but even in my youthful state of untapped prophetic potential, I just knew what I knew.

I moped through the rest of the school year. For the first time in my life, I was totally emotionally invested in a relationship. I was faced with the responsibility of ending my connection with the girl back home and I didn't know how to do it. I wasn't going home for the summer because I was already committed to playing drums and traveling with one of the summer music ministry teams. I didn't want to write a letter. I wanted to tell her face-to-face.

Carol had the team's itinerary and a letter was waiting for me in nearly every city. We wrote long passionate letters to one another and we still have them to this day. Sometimes we take them out and read them and it's a fantastic way to rekindle the fire.

My hometown was our last stop for the music team's tour and I was faced with the daunting task of breaking the news to my old girl friend. She actually attended the concert, which was performed in my home church.

It was a weird night from start to finish. The team members were really confused and surprised when they saw me sitting with her and my friends, because they had only seen me with Carol all during the school year. I was certain that they were assuming that I had been "playing" between two girls.

I did end the relationship and she was very angry. However the scope of the whole situation changed dramatically when a few months later, my younger sister called to inform me that my old flame was pregnant. Of course, a few of the home church folks suspected me, but that was physically impossible. I hadn't even been in town for several months. We had never been sexually intimate. I was very much, a virgin. Man, how did my life become so filled with drama?

When I got back to school, I moved in with my brother Mark and we became roommates. Imagine your older brother allowing you to be his roommate in his last year of college.

I felt very special. He was the first one in my family to learn of the true nature of my relationship with Carol. He was very supportive in what proved to be a very trying semester.

First, I was hit with new financial pressure as the tuition almost doubled. I only had enough financial aid to make it through one more semester without being forced to borrow more money.

Then tragedy struck the campus. One of the young women, a member of the very popular campus choir and ensemble for which I played drums, died in her sleep. I had never experienced the death of a friend. Growing up in church, I saw older people die and heard about young people dying, but it had never been this close.

I was emotionally blown away. I was spiritually blown away. For the first time in my life, I began to question God, and all my beliefs and values. I simply caved in. I literally felt something inside of me crumbling. I was unable to focus so I discontinued my education. I dropped out of school midway through the spring 1979 term and found myself in a state of depression over all these disappointments in my life.

Meanwhile, Carol and I wrote letters and ran up huge long distance telephone bills. By the summer of 1979, we were back together. She had worked and saved enough money to get back to Tulsa, and was able to move in with a friend who lived off campus. Even though she could not attend school, we were united again.

This caused a major rift between Carol and her mother. We didn't realize how much this was affecting our parents. It tears a parent apart to see their children make rash emotional decisions that can cost them their lives.

We worked in all kinds of situations in order to be together. We worked fast food, retail sales, a phone bank, and I took various temporary assignments like: yard work, hauling and factory labor. We did whatever we had to do because we had a goal to one day get married and be together for keeps.

24

After a few months, we were able to escape from living with family and friends, as each of us got our own places. That was a dangerous move because it gave us plenty of time to be alone.

Passion was high and there was lots of fondling and going too far. The only thing that stopped us from going all the way was the fact that we KNEW Carol would get pregnant. There was no doubt in our minds about that, but still we went way too far since we were not married. We don't mean to be coarse or offensive, but we must be frank.

Many Christian couples are on this path today, so we have to let them know that we've been there, too. Many nights I left Carol's place at three O'clock in the morning. Sometimes I stayed all night and dashed off to work the next morning. It's amazing how much stamina you have when you're young and stupid.

It was a season in which two young adults had their first taste of freedom from parental control and church boundaries. We were living on pure emotions and desperation. Today, we fully understand the couple that clings to what feels like their once in a lifetime chance to experience love. We understand why they abandon their values and morals for the temporary feeling of physical oneness.

We were, as some denominations of the Christian Church call, backslidden. As far as we were concerned, it was Chris and Carol against the world. We isolated ourselves from family and friends and just lived in the moment.

I finally got a steady job with Radio Shack and I was doing well as a salesman since electronic gadgets and technical stuff was my specialty. Carol worked in a jewelry store and was getting expert training in that field. That's when I decided to ask her to marry me. During the fall of 1979, I began saving toward the purchase of a promise/ engagement ring. Once I made the purchase, I made my plans to give it to her for Christmas.

I asked her what she wanted for Christmas and she told me that she needed some boots, so that gave me an idea on how to propose to her.

I put the ring inside of a box and placed that box inside of a slightly larger box. I placed each box inside of a larger box until I had one big box that would appear to be the right size to contain a pair of boots.

On Christmas Day of 1979, I was exhausted and excited. I had gotten home very late the night before due to the madness of the last day of holiday shopping. I went to Carol's place, which was actually a one-room efficiency apartment.

I brought my big gift-wrapped box. I could tell that she was sure that it was a pair of boots. I gave it to her and watched her unwrap and open the first box. She had a real puzzled look on her face as she uncovered another box. With each box, she was more curious and I still suspect that she had a pretty good idea what was going on by the time she got down to the last box.

She laughed before she opened it. I got down on one knee and asked her to marry me. She cried. She laughed. She cried. We embraced and kissed.

Carol recalls the proposal: *We had asked each other what each would like for Christmas. Chris needed a wallet and I asked for a pair of boots. When the time came to exchange gifts, I gave him his gift and watched him open it. He gave me mine and I KNEW it was boots. The box was wrapped in Christmas paper and big enough for boots so when he handed it to me the only thing on my mind was that I wondered what they looked like.*

I tore off the wrapping paper and opened the box and inside it was another box. I looked at him and just laughed wondering what he was up to. I just figured he decided to buy something else. I was a little disappointed, but still excited about what it could be. I opened the next box and inside of it was another box and the idea began to dawn on me that it could be a ring.

I thought to myself, "No, it's a present, not a ring." so that I wouldn't be disappointed in case it wasn't.

I kept opening boxes until I reached a jewelry box. I looked at him and started laughing and crying. Chris got down on one knee and asked me to marry him as I opened the box to see my engagement ring. I said yes, we hugged, kissed and cried together.

***

We moved into the New Year of 1980 with more hopes and dreams for a life and future together. Life was very difficult, but we always found comfort in each other's arms. However, we were still dealing with the nagging conviction from the Holy Spirit concerning our inappropriate physical contact because we knew we were living outside of the values we had been taught.

One weekend we heard a preacher/ teacher present a message that talked about the deeds of sin being accomplished even if it was only done in the heart, the same way it is when a man looks at a woman with lust in his heart. We felt convicted about how we were living, but we didn't stop. We thought that since we didn't go all the way, we weren't committing any serious sin. Besides, we were going to get married anyway.

Around that same time, in March of 1980, we had our first life threatening encounter and the realization of why you cannot play around with sin in your life.

On March 25, 1980 a drunk driver ran a red light and crashed into us as we drove through an intersection. He plowed into our car, flipping us upside down. Really, we were upside down with the engine still running. After the world finally stopped spinning, for a few seconds we were still in our seats even though we were not wearing seat belts. Somehow we were held in place. Then, gravity slowly kicked in and we slid out of our seats. Out of the silence, Carol calmly said,

"Chris, turn the engine off."

People came out of nowhere and began to pull us out of the vehicle. There were fire trucks, police cars, an ambulance and flashing lights everywhere. We were very much in shock because everything was a blur.

When the fire crew turned the car over and set it back on its wheels, gasoline poured out from the exact spot from where we had been hit. The collision had ruptured the gas tank. It was proof that there should have been an explosion and we should have been dead. God used the accident to turn our lives right side up. We knew it was time to make things right.

First, we got together and prayed, repenting before the Lord. We asked him for a fresh start. We also made plans for me to go back to college so that at least one of us would be academically prepared for our future together.

We received a very nice financial settlement from the car accident and we used part of the money to secure a better apartment for Carol while I prepared to get back into college life. Our goal was for me to finish my education while Carol worked. After my graduation, we would get married, I would work and she would go to school.

With the help of my eldest brother Raphael, who called on a favor from a friend, I was able to get back into school in the fall of 1980. However, one month into the new school year, I received a phone call from a collection agency demanding payments on my student loans even though I was re-enrolled.

I just couldn't handle the pressure when I got unexpected demands like that. It was one of those things that we didn't realize was a serious red flag in a fiancée, and this response to life was going to raise its ugly head again. I was only 21 years old and I snapped. I quit school again.

We aborted our original plans, went through some premarital sessions with a local pastor and within three months, got married.

Promise

Skeletons Out of the Closet

The first months of marriage were great. First of all, we didn't have to restrain ourselves anymore. We always regretted getting sexually involved at inappropriate levels before marriage, but since we always stopped short of actual intercourse, we were very glad that we had at least preserved the full experience for marriage.

In the prior weeks and months of total physical abstinence, it made us anticipate and appreciate the gift of sex and how precious it really is in the context of marriage. Sex is better within marriage. There's no guilt, shame, remorse, fear or apprehension attached to it.

At first, it seemed like this marriage thing was much easier than all the warnings had led us to believe. Carol's mother hadn't been happy with her only daughter running off to marry some young buck from the Midwest and my parents had given me some thorough interrogation, too.

Parents can be intensely afraid that their children will make the same mistakes that they made. I was the first of my parent's children to get married. I was ahead of my older siblings. Since I was the quiet middle child, this was a shock to everyone. Carol was a first-born child and the only girl in her family, so this was equally a shock to them as well.

In his first real man-to-man talk with me about my decision, my dad told me that Carol reminded him of his first wife. I was like, *"First, what?"*

"O' yeah," he explained, "I never told you that your mother is my second wife."

Man, marriage has a way of bringing skeletons out of the closet for everybody, not just the happy, oblivious couple. My dad went on to disclose how his first wife cheated on him with his best friend. He just wanted to make sure that I knew what I was getting myself into.

On the other side, Carol's mother was very afraid that her only daughter was getting married just to escape from her family and the extremely low probability of fulfilling her dreams in Harrisburg, Pennsylvania. She knew, first hand, the danger of getting married just to escape your home situation.

After twelve years of marriage, her husband (Carol's dad) walked away. Carol's parents got married just to escape their homes and neither was ready for the tons of psychological and emotional baggage that each brought into the relationship. Now it appeared that their little girl was about to do the same thing.

We were the typical couple who thought, *"Well, that's not going to be our story because we LOVE each other."*

Funny how that strong emotional love doesn't cover issues like one person preferring the room warm and other preferring the room cool. One person likes to sleep with a night light and the other wants total darkness. Emotional love doesn't seem to cover the annoying scraping sound of a fork against teeth or the bothersome slurping sounds when the other person drinks. It doesn't seem to have the power to deal with bad breath, body odor and the dreaded menstrual cycle. It seems to crumble in the face of one of the most highly exalted declarations of all, *"That's not how I was taught to do it!"*

For the first five months, we were sailing, but all of a sudden, there was cold silence from my wife. I had no idea why she was shutting down. I thought things were okay, but I didn't know I was offending and frightening her.

If I made a suggestion, she would go silent. If we were about to argue about something she would stop talking. I was totally stomped. What in the world did I say? What in the world did I do? I couldn't get her to engage in a conflict. If I disagreed with something she said or did, I let her know. But I couldn't get her to tell me what I had said or done to cause her to go silent.

In the Green family, we fight! We hash it out. We talk it out. No matter how long it takes, nobody can leave the room until this issue is resolved. So why couldn't I get this girl to talk to me anymore. I was frustrated. I was lost.

Carol recalls: *Not only was it matter of not talking, but I didn't have the words to express what I wanted to say. I also had a fear of having an argument. For me, arguments led to separation because that's what I saw. That's how I summed it up from what happened in my house growing up. I saw arguments as something that led to parents not being together. So I would shut down, not because I was trying to be manipulative, but because I was afraid.*

***

"It's not supposed to be like this."
The first real problems that a couple encounters are very, very difficult to deal with. All you know is that it's not supposed to be like this. That's one of the thoughts that will become a seed of doubt in the heart if you dwell on it. This thought is closely connected with "I deserve to be happy" which is even more dangerous because it supposes that your spouse is responsible for your happiness. It also supposes that you have a RIGHT to be happy and if your spouse is doing something to take away your happiness then you have the right to do whatever it takes to get your happiness back.

There's a lot of selfishness embedded in those thoughts. On a subliminal, nonverbal level, we're communicating some awfully negative and hurtful messages regardless of our intentions. Even when all you're trying to do is figure out what you are doing wrong, the message that comes across to your spouse can be an accusation of all the things that are wrong with them.

It wasn't long before I played out all the possible scenarios in my head, of where this was going to end and I realized that this was a no-win situation.

"Maybe we made a mistake."
When you come to the place where you feel boxed into a corner and you cannot resolve the situation, the ultimate conclusion is that you have made a mistake in getting into the situation in the first place. That's one of the heart stabbers.

Many couples come to this conclusion after a few years of trial and error in the marriage. We were getting close to that conclusion after a few months of marriage. Remember, we had known each other for three and a half years before we got married. We were actually four years into the relationship even though it was only five months into the marriage.

We had stood before a judge and stood before a pastor, taking those sacred vows twice, but it was beginning to feel like this was not going to work.

Kindergarten Basics

We love the ministry of Dr. Gary Chapman and how he addresses the five love languages in his excellent book. It has helped us to understand one another in powerful ways, but in the early years of Chris and Carol Green, before we could advance to understand love languages, we had to go all the way back to kindergarten basics.

Somehow it began to occur to us that the reason we could not communicate was not only because we didn't have the same language, but also because we didn't have the same words. We didn't even have the same alphabet.

My A was not the same as her A.
My B was not the same as her B.
My C was not the same as her C.

If our letters were not the same, then certainly our spelling wasn't the same. If our spelling wasn't the same, then our words were not the same.

Carol described our barrier like this: *We were like two people coming from different countries and cultures who didn't speak the same language. We could make gestures, but we still didn't really know one another's culture from which our language developed. It wasn't until we got married that this difference came to the surface.*

***

No matter how sincerely we were trying to communicate, we could not connect. Words, phrases and actions said something different to her than what I was meaning. Words, phrases and actions said something different to me than what she was meaning.

Even this realization was not enough, though. For about a month we thought that this understanding was enough to carry us through, but it wasn't. Knowing we had a problem was not helping us with the problem.

There had to be a way to stay connected with one another while we engaged in this process of understanding one another's alphabet, words and languages.

The PACT

We cannot recall the exact date and time, but following another one of those frustrating moments of futility, we sat down together to try to reach some agreed place from which we could deal with one another. It was really out of desperation that we came up with an agreement. We weren't trying to be deep or spiritual. We were just trying to find some common ground.

So we made a PACT and it went something like this:

I choose to believe that no matter how you say, what you say to me, **that you are not intentionally trying to hurt me**.

I choose to believe that no matter how you say, what you say to me, **that you meant it for my good**.

I choose to believe that no matter how you say, what you say to me, **that you love me**.

When we made this PACT, we had no idea how significant it was going to be. We just felt a new sense of peace. It was like we were finally, really married. We had slowly moved beyond the soaring emotional connections of love and advanced to a solid unconditional acceptance of one another.

We had a new security. We had tapped into a secret place from where we could begin learning one another's alphabet; and thus begin to piece together words and sentences. Simultaneously, we could build a stronger connection between us. It was like working on our health while working on an injury at the same time.

Sometimes our family and friends comment on our present ability to communicate in a manner that seems almost telepathic. We can just say one word or give a brief glance across a room and we are able to conduct an entire conversation in a few seconds.

This level of communication began when a couple that had only been married for six months, in a moment of desperation, made a PACT in a little apartment in Tulsa, Oklahoma.

Years of Open Confession
We don't want to convey the wrong idea about our three and a half years prior to marriage. There was a lot more than just strong emotional and sexual attraction. We had countless hours of talking and confession of things about ourselves that we had never disclosed to anyone. We just had no idea how those things would affect us after we got married.

We confessed how we both had struggled with the secret thing many teenagers do behind closed doors. As a very young child of about three or four years old, a neighborhood boy coerced me into the basement of the two-family flat in which we lived. I had no idea what he was doing to me. I just knew that I didn't like it and it felt very dirty.

Carol, as an adolescent, had a girl attempt to lure her into a sexual encounter. Just like me, she just knew that she didn't like it. When you go to those depths of openness with someone, it was no wonder that we became soul mates and partners in crime.

By the time we got married, we knew almost everything imaginable about one another. We had confessed the deepest and darkest of secrets. Even with that, we still were not prepared for the relational maze that is marriage.

Our PACT gave us a new starting point that was beyond the sharing of similar experiences, hurts and struggles. It changed our interaction. We discovered the ability to move beyond the initial reaction of irritation, anger and silence that always led to a standoff.

Carol recalls: *Before our PACT, I heard whatever he said to me as criticism. Even though we made the PACT, I still had to make a choice. We still had to walk it out.*

For instance I had a real bad problem with procrastination. If something needed to be done, like making an important phone call, I would keep putting it off. When he would remind me to make the phone call, it triggered my insecurity. The real issue was that I wasn't sure of what to say and how to come back with the right answers in case I was asked certain questions.

Before our PACT, it never occurred to me to just simply admit, 'I don't know what to say'. I learned that he was willing to help me and teach me how to handle the phone calls. I had never had that kind of support before. I never had anyone pulling out of me what I was thinking.

Our PACT took away the nonverbal accusation that he thought I was incompetent. I saw that it was me; that I just didn't know how to approach the phone situation. I didn't know how to handle it, but he knew how to handle it and was willing to teach me. And this opened up a whole new aspect to our relationship. He had what I did not have in this arena of public interaction and I chose to receive it. I chose not to respond in pride and be stupid about it. I chose to receive what he was giving to me.

***

During that first marriage impasse, we never considered divorce. That was the last thing on our minds. I had already quit higher education twice. Back in high school I had quit football, soccer and my dream of becoming a scientist. I was tired of being a quitter. Carol had failed in her pursuit of a college degree. If we could not be successful at anything else in life, we wanted to be a good husband and wife. We could not give up on our marriage.

Equal Responsibility
When you make the type of agreement that we made in our PACT, it places the responsibility on both people. Just think about it. We had just agreed that no matter what the other person spoke, that we would choose to believe that they meant it for what was best for our marriage. We would choose to believe that what was said was out of genuine love.

The weight of that agreement was not just on the person who was choosing to believe that they were loved, but it also required honesty and integrity on the other person to never move into manipulating. We could never use this agreement to intimidate the other person. We could never attempt to dominate the other person.

You see it would have been very easy to manipulate, intimidate or dominate Carol because I could assume that she was going to believe what I said to be coming from a motivation of love. She could do the same to me. However we could also fall into the trap of always testing the other person to see if what they were doing or saying was being faked.

The only way our PACT could work was if we both took the risk of honoring every aspect of it. Neither of us could be overly concerned or wondering if the other person was doing their part. If we did that, the PACT would not work. This was the basic foundation that we laid so that we could move on in our marriage.

At one point in our lives we were hosting a pre-marital preparation class in our local church. In every class, we would talk about our PACT and challenge couples to use this kind of commitment to determine if they were ready for marriage.

The Prescription for Healing

In Psalm 119 a very special word appears throughout the passage. The writer says things *like I long for your precepts* or *I will keep your precepts*.

In our studies, we learned that this word, **precept**, is closely related to our modern word for prescription. It means God has given us a special visitation to make a very thorough examination and based upon what He sees, He gives a set of regulations for us to follow that will bring healing.

This is the same concept of a physician who gives us a medical examination and based upon what he or she discovers in our bodies, they write out a prescription that will bring healing to that condition.

That's what our PACT became for us. It was a set of precepts; a prescription that God gave us to bring healing to our marriage. Now, you can see why the Psalmist would say, *Behold, I long for your precepts.* It's like saying, "Lord, I long for Your visitations because You're going to speak to me and heal me with Your Word."

Today, we are able to look back and see why the PACT worked for us. We didn't know how to explain it while we were living it, but now we have the words to articulate at least three precepts that emerged from it. These precepts can help a couple build and sustain a long and happy marriage. They can help an individual build and sustain lasting relationships.

To help us successfully communicate these precepts, we converted the word PACT into an acronym: **P**romise of **A**ccountability, **C**ommitment and **T**rust.

It just kind of rolls off the tongue when you say it out loud, doesn't it? It sounds really clever, but we have to be totally honest with you and tell you that we aint smart enough to come up with anything like this. Only the Holy Spirit of God can plant a seed into your heart, nurture it for thirty years and then reveal His wisdom by giving you an acronym to explain the precepts that were applied in your life. Wow! God gets all the Glory!

We didn't learn these things in a sequential or chronological order. God didn't say, "I'm going to teach you about accountability for tens years, and then commitment for ten years and then trust for ten years."

These precepts were woven into the fabric of our marriage. Through every fight and love making night, we were following these Godly prescriptions. Throughout the childbearing years and the endless tears, we were following these Godly prescriptions. Through victories great and small, and when nothing seemed to be happening at all, we were following these Godly prescriptions.

Marriage is not the pinnacle
We realize this book is going to be read by many people who have already experienced the pain of separation and divorce. What can they take away from this conversation?

Divorce is a psychosocial loss that leaves two individuals and their families agonizing through a grieving process. Depending upon the school of thought, they will deal with 5-7 stages of grief that include shock, denial, bargaining, saddness and anger.

If you have been divorced, we encourage you to resist the temptation to attach negative philosophies to your outlook on future relationships. You must also resist the temptation to apply personal interpretation of the Bible by changing the meaning of the scripture to fit your feelings. Otherwise, you will repeat the pattern, all the while thinking the problems are not with you, but with your new companion or spouse.

From this point in your life, please proceed slowly. Take your time. Healing takes time. If you should choose to enter a serious relationship again, you cannot apply self-preservation tactics. Of course, that is going to be very tough because of what you've gone through, but unless you learn how to make a PACT with yourself and GOD, you will inevitably end up in another break up. It will happen for different reasons than before, but it will still be the same results as before.

As high as the divorce and separation rates are, they're even higher for people who are on their second marriage. Why? We believe it's because they attempt to make it work without really understanding what happened the first time and the affect that it has had on their heart and mind.

As you have discovered, marriage is not the ultimate pinnacle of all of life's experiences. It can be a special part of God's plan for your life, but it is not the goal of your life. Our word of comfort to you is that God still has a great plan for you.

The intent of the PACT precepts, for the divorcee, is that they would become like a surgeon's tool in God's hand. You are about to undergo major surgery that will mend you from the inside out. Someone reading this book has been torn so badly that you feel like your heart was ripped from your chest with no anesthesia to ease the pain.

As you read the precepts of the PACT, please know that we are not pushing you back into marriage, but God is using this sensitive topic to do a mighty healing and cleansing work inside of you.

You will no longer avoid the subject of marriage and seeing other couples will not bring tears to your eyes. Instead, you will be motivated to live out the purpose of God for your life, if whether it includes marriage or not.

That's what we want you to take away from this conversation.

A healthy view and understanding of marriage
Before you turn another page and begin to take this journey with us, put aside your highlighter or notepad and just pause for a moment. This is not a book packed with strategies on how to make your marriage successful; nor is it a manual from which to make notes and attempt to replicate our life experiences in your situation. We didn't write this book to help you discover how to find a husband or wife. The purpose behind this book can be perceived in two Bible scriptures:

For whatever things were written before, were written for our learning, that we through the patience and comfort of the scriptures might have hope.
(Romans 15:4, NKJV)

Wisdom is the most important thing; so get wisdom. If it costs everything you have, get understanding.
(Proverbs 4:7, New Century Version)

We realize that a lot of what we are about to share is going to sound out of date, irrelevant and even sexist according to the standards and beliefs of the 21st century world. Most of the people we have been teaching in our weekly church gatherings are divorced, separated, presently having marital trouble, or single. This book is NOT meant to bring condemnation on anyone due to the life status they may be in right now. We just want to 'keep it real' with transparency and present the truth, in love.

We are not saying that everyone MUST be married. We are not saying that everyone SHOULD be married. Yet, we are saying that everyone MUST and SHOULD have a healthy view and understanding of marriage.

You are not going to get that healthy view from the media. It won't come from the Oprah Winfrey Network (OWN), Essence Magazine, Black Entertainment Television (BET) or Lifetime Television. You won't get it from the latest music videos.

A healthy view of marriage is not in the agenda of Planned Parenthood or the National Organization for Women. You won't get it from your friends who are content with the online Urban Dictionary definition of **ghetto love**: *that kinda luv where...yall cut each other's throat that nite at the club wit your pocket knives for lookin at otha people ...then the next morning she hanging over his shoulders bragging about how in love they are...*

We are not marriage counselors and we are not professional therapists. All we know is that we have followed the principles and precepts of the Word of God in our relationship and we are still happy together. We have weathered job losses, two foreclosures, emergency (near-death) hospital crisis moments, infidelity temptation, full time ministry overload, and the on-going challenge of parenting. We have clung to one another in tragedies and laughed together in triumphs. We are not flawless and we still have our emotional and economic issues in life, but our relationship and our family remain intact.

We are not boasting in ourselves, but we are boasting about the validity and assurance of God's Word (The Bible). There are many others in your community and across the nation, who will testify of this truth and reality. For the thousands of people who may question our beliefs and our lifestyle, they simply cannot argue with our results.

Love and Respect
The underlying principles of our PACT came down to this: Husband, love your wife. Wife, respect your husband. We have found that the requirement for each of us cuts to the very core of the heart. It's very easy for a man to withhold love and it's very easy for a woman to refuse respect. These responses are due to human nature's will to preserve itself whenever faced with destruction, disappointment, doubt, division or discouragement.

We have learned through some of the marriage ministries from whom we received help, like Dr. Dennis Rainey, that the goal in marriage is Christ-likeness for a husband and Christ-likeness for a wife. That's what it takes in order for a man to love his wife the way Christ loves the church. That's what it takes for a woman to submit to and respect her husband.

If we try to approach marriage and relationships with the standards of this generation, like ME FIRST, PRENUPTUAL AGREEMENTS, MAKING SURE I WON'T BE LEFT IN THE COLD, WHAT ARE YOU GOING TO DO FOR ME? and WHAT DO I GET OUT OF THIS?, then we will continue to see high divorce rates or more couples choosing to just live together and not get married at all.

There is a lot of hurt and pain that's deeply rooted in our hearts and it's very difficult to sort it all out when dealing with one another. This understanding went a long way in helping us in our moments of crisis, conflict and confrontation.

That's why, as we disclose the precepts that we have learned from the PACT, we first want to connect you to the promises of Isaiah 61, verses 1 and 4:

"The Spirit of the Lord GOD is upon Me, Because the LORD has anointed Me to preach good tidings to the poor; He has sent Me to heal the brokenhearted, To proclaim liberty to the captives, And the opening of the prison to those who are bound; ...And they shall rebuild the old ruins, they shall raise up the former desolations, and they shall repair the ruined cities, the desolations of many generations."

Our prayer is that as we address the issues within marriage, you will be able to more accurately apply the true meaning of Isaiah 61 in very practical ways to your own heart and home.

In the church community in which we are leading, we have chosen to seriously deal with the foundation of the family, which is marriage. The reason it is so difficult to talk about it is because most of our audience consists of people from the urban community who have been wounded in some way or another due to the breakdown in their marriage or their family. Most have grown up without a father, mother, or in a few cases, without both.

We have discerned that when we talk about this subject, we must be sensitive and gentle because there are a lot of sore spots, even within the Christian community. It is very easy for some people to walk away from our sessions struggling with thoughts of condemnation or offense, but the Lord has been helping us to teach and present a loving view of our heavenly Father regarding marriage and relationships.

A Biblical Foundation
The PACT is deeply rooted in sound doctrine. It can be summed up in Ephesians 5:31-33:

"For this reason a man shall leave his father and mother and be joined to his wife, and the two shall become one flesh. This

is a great mystery, but I speak concerning Christ and the church. Nevertheless let each one of you in particular so love his own wife as himself, and let the wife see that she respects her husband."

Today, in America, many men are strongly opposed to this command to love their wives the same way Christ loves the church. Many women almost consider words like *submit* and *respect* to be profanity. In the face of a society that pushes individuality and personal success, we are under divine mandate to present God's point of view about marriage.

We guess we are still some of those 'old school' folks who believe that the foundation of the community is the family, and the foundation of the family is the marriage relationship between a man and woman. To take it a step further, we are not convinced that it takes a village to raise a child. We believe that it takes a family to raise a child, and that child's family upbringing works best where there is a married father and mother. We are not condemning anyone who cannot provide that for their child. Life happens. That's why we wrote this book.

We didn't say that you don't have a family if you don't have a mom or dad present in the home. We're just stating what GOD had in mind when HE started everything in the beginning. Certainly God has graced many families to thrive as the remaining spouse pressed forward for the sake of the children. But for the sake of this discussion, we are dealing with the intended foundation of the family; which is marriage.

While many are tweaking and adjusting the terms of marriage to fit their own preferences and lifestyles, we feel that we must lovingly and firmly present the truth of God's Word.

If a marriage fails, you don't discard the fundamental institution of marriage, no more than one would refuse to ever drive a car again because it had a flat tire, or if the battery dies. You repair what went wrong and you keep driving. If the car runs out of gas, you don't give up on all cars. You do whatever you have to do in order to get some more fuel into it again. You wouldn't say *"I don't believe in automobiles because they break down and you have to keep refueling them."*

However, this society declares that since so many marriages have failed, we no longer need the institution of marriage or if you decide to get married, you don't need to apply all that spiritual stuff in the relationship. Many couples approach marriage like a very loose boyfriend-girlfriend connection. At the first sign of trouble, they have already created all kinds of escape routes.

Then there are the countless situations where one person simply gives up on the marriage, leaving the other one deeply wounded from the rejection. We can't imagine any harsher words than to hear the person to whom you once pledged your life say, "I don't love you anymore."

One or both people feeling taken for granted usually precede this declaration. Misunderstandings pile up as unresolved conflicts build walls between them. Emotionally there are major disconnections as the relationship slowly dies. We were certainly starting down that path as newlyweds.

One of our very good friends, Pastor Joe Green of Antioch Assembly in Harrisburg, PA, shared that he learned that one of the Hebrew word-pictures for marriage is that of a couple being barricaded inside of a house with no way to escape. If there is a fire, they have to work together to put out the fire, not try to find a way to get out of the house.

As radical as that may sound, that's how marriage works. It's not about self-preservation. It's about doing whatever it takes for US to make it, not just for ME to make it. BOTH people must make the promise of accountability, commitment and trust.

Accountability

It's Not My Fault

We have watched athletes, entertainers, politicians and preachers who have held press conferences to acknowledge infidelity in their marriage. Their admissions have been followed by huge swells of public flogging and analysis as we place them on trial to judge and execute them.

After a few weeks, the hype settles down and we go back to dealing with our own lives, relationships and marriages that in many cases are in the same shambles as the high profile personality that we have condemned.

As we conduct self-diagnosis regarding the health of our relationships, we find it a lot easier to play a secret blame game and summarize everything with a simple conclusion, *"It's not my fault."* We find it easy to minimize our contribution to the rift in the relationship while we magnify what our mate has said and done.

Explainable and Answerable

The secret blame game is a major problem in marriage and we think of it as being like quicksand. You're in it before you know it and the more you struggle, the faster you go down.

How do you reach a place of healing and restoration so that you can get out of blame game? For us, it started with the precept (prescription) of accountability. This precept helped us recognize the quicksand because it introduced us to the value and principle of being accountable to one another.

A basic definition of accountability is: willingness to accept responsibility for one's own actions and words. More specifically, it means that BOTH the husband and wife are willing to keep themselves in the position where they are explainable to one another.

This precept involved a promise that we would always keep ourselves in the position where we would be willing to explain why I did what I did, or why I said what I said. It was a promise that we would be answerable to one another.

Be Honest With Yourself

A lot of couples don't keep themselves in the position to be explainable to one another. They often keep themselves in the position where they can easily hide, duck, dodge and avoid the real issues surrounding their conflict.

This is a behavioral pattern that a person brings into the relationship. One person or the other (sometimes both) have always been able to avoid bill collectors, relatives, obligations, and task. Some have elevated their ability to avoid responsibility to an art form. It can be very painful to find yourself living with someone who always keeps themselves in a position where they don't have to answer your questions or explain their actions. It's very difficult to stay connected with someone like that.

When it comes to the precept of accountability, we are talking about a self-imposed obligation to be honest with your mate. First of all it forces you to be honest with yourself. You'll find that a lot of people, who won't be accountable to their spouse, won't even be accountable to themselves. They won't be honest with themselves about how they feel and about what they are doing. The reason they won't answer their mate's questions is because they won't answer their own questions. They won't answer their own conscience, even when it is speaking to them and saying things like, *"You know what you're doing is wrong. You know what you're saying is wrong."* They block out their internal moral gauge.

That's why the first thing that was established in our PACT was THE PROMISE OF ACCOUNTABILITY. To understand this precept we need to walk through a passage of scripture that has left many people frustrated because of the inability to live out the interpretation they've been handed.

Follow the Leader

Ephesians 5:22-24 says, *Wives, submit to your own husbands, as to the Lord. For the husband is head of the wife, as also Christ is head of the church; and He is the Savior of the body. Therefore, just as the church is subject to Christ, so let the wives be to their own husbands in everything.*

Ephesians 5:33 - *Nevertheless let each one of you in particular so love his own wife as himself, and let the wife see that she respects her husband.*

We can almost feel the cold chill sweeping over many of you, but hold on! This is not going to be the typical law enforcement approach to this scripture.

The on-going battle has always been about who will make the first move. Husbands will declare such things as, *"I'll show her love when she shows me respect."* Wives have stood their ground at, *"I'll respect him when he shows me love."*

For thousands of years men and women have faced off at this ancient impasse, with no one willing to make the first move. We believe that the husband needs to make the first move, but let us give you the reason why we take this position.

First, we need to explain the meanings of these words in terms that people can relate to today. Phrases like *"head of the wife"* need to be stated another way to help both sides get the right picture. Basically this means that husbands are instructed to take the lead and set the example for their home as they follow the lead of Christ, who has set the example for the church.

Christ is the husband's lead and example. Christ made the first move. He loved us and died for us while we were still sinners. So just like Christ, husbands should make the first move.

To the wives: All the controversy and fuss about words like *submit* and *subject* can be boiled down to this basic explanation. These words mean that wives are to follow their husband's lead. It's that simple.

To lead means to be the first to do something. Husbands are called to be the first to love, the first to sacrifice, the first to give, the first to pray, the first to ask for help, and the first to (fill in the blank). So when your husband leads out in loving, sacrificing, giving, praying, etc, you are called to follow his lead and do the same thing that he is doing. In fact ladies, even though your husband has authority, you carry the ability. God grants him the right to do a thing and grants you the ability to help him get it done. In this way, you are doing things together.

A Real Man of God
We have heard many women say that they wanted a real man of God, but then they learn that a real man of God might say, *"Let's turn off the TV so we can talk and pray about our finances."* or *"I believe the Lord wants us to fast about what's going on in our child's school."*

She discovers the challenge in following a man who is led by Christ. He always seems to want to talk, fast or pray at the most inconvenient times. God is always telling him to do things that yank her out of her comfort and security zone.

So, it's really about submitting to her husband's leadership. As her husband is following the leading of the Spirit of God, she is called to unite with him and not resist it.

Of course, this automatically brings up the issue of what are husbands to do when their wives do not follow their lead. Well, husbands are instructed to love their wives anyway; the way Christ loves the church. He is called to wash her with the water of the word. There are reasons why she is unwilling to follow her husband's lead. Those reasons can range from fear to rebellion. However, the husband has the high calling of God on his life to minister to his wife. We'll talk about this again later in the book.

Trust God, Don't Be Afraid
The other side of the coin is: What does a wife do if her husband is not setting an example and following Christ? Well, Peter dealt with that issue and instructed that when this happens, wives are to follow the example of Christ, as well.

According to 1 Peter 3:1-4, a wife may be able to win her husband without words or her outward beauty. Peter wrote, *"...rather let it be the hidden person of the heart, with the incorruptible beauty of a gentle and quiet spirit, which is very precious in the sight of God."*

When a husband is not following the Lord, fear of the consequences of his actions can overwhelm his wife. Her fear is often rooted in past experiences with him or other men. This fear can cause her to say and do things she shouldn't.

Many Bible teachers have put emphasis on the wife having a gentle and quiet spirit, but they sometimes fail to tell her how to do it. We believe that this is developed over time as a woman matures in the ways of God.

A wife can grow and mature to a place where she has a gentle, quiet spirit that speaks volumes. Interestingly, Peter told the wives that they should do what the women of past times did which was to:
   1.) trust God
   2.) do good, and
   3.) do not respond in fear.

*For in this manner, in former times, the holy women **who trusted in God** also adorned themselves, being submissive to their own husbands, as Sarah obeyed Abraham, calling him lord, whose daughters you are **if you do good and are not afraid with any terror.*** (1 Peter 3: 5-6, NKJV)

From this you can see how she is able to develop this inner strength. Gentle and quiet is not weakness. It is the powerful expression of meekness. Meekness is having the strength to control oneself.

Please note that a quiet spirit does not necessarily mean that she's a quiet person. There are many Godly women who have a lot to say, but it comes from a gentle, quiet spirit. Anybody can blow up and let everyone around them know that they got strength, skills, talent and smarts. Blasting your thoughts and opinions is no sign of being a strong person.

If she learns to trust God and receive His perfect love, it will casts out her fear, and her husband's words and actions won't be able to continually cause her to react. She won't allow herself to become an instrument in the hands of the evil one.

Today, many women in the urban community are filling their hearts and minds with fear by watching constant streams of men-bashing movies, dramatic presentations and talk shows. The fear factor is sky rocketing, causing millions of women to take matters into their own hands. Many are turning to lesbian relationships for comfort and security.

Husbands and wives, please hear us! Your words and actions have a deep impact on your mate's emotional and psychological state. You may not be aware of the reality that they need to be delivered from strongholds like REJECTION and FEAR. Your words and deeds can either hinder or assist with their deliverance.

Laying a New Foundation
Not long after we made our PACT, we moved from Tulsa, Oklahoma to St. Louis, Missouri. It was the start of a season of getting somewhat back on track. We worked hard and found a small apartment as we settled into daily life.

We spent a lot of time just learning each other. We would explain what we meant when we used certain phrases and terms. It was fascinating as we realized the differences in our backgrounds. Carol was from a small east coast town. Chris was from a large Midwest city. Even though we shared similar interest and ideas, our views of the world and life had been shaped by our upbringing. During our first two years in St. Louis, we were really working hard at building this new communication foundation.

In February of 1983 we began traveling and providing administrative help for my brother, Raphael Green and his evangelistic campaigns. We temporarily set aside our personal plans to help him build and fortify the ministry, Love Reach, Inc. (to be later known as Metro Associates). It's amazing how God can use you even when you're still a work in progress.

Five months later we returned to St. Louis after Ray (as we called him) got married and moved to Virginia. We were in limbo as we started looking for new jobs and a place to live. One of our best friends asked us to move back to Tulsa, but we eventually settled into the direction that we had peace about for our lives, which meant staying in St. Louis and living with my parents until we found jobs.

And did we ever find jobs! We found great jobs! We finally got paid! But we compromised the purpose of God for salaries and benefits. We launched forth in our quest to fulfill the American dream, which is really the American fantasy.

Chasing the Fantasy
For nearly three years (1983-1986) things were seemingly successful. We progressed from renting an apartment to buying a house. We financed two cars. Around June of 1985 Carol revealed she was expecting our first child. Life was good, even though our priorities were off.

We joined a good church, but I was so buried in my new career in financial services that I sporadically gave time and money to the ministry. Sometimes I was very diligent and faithful. Most times I was working toward fulfilling the dream.

Then our world crashed in March of 1986. Carol's employment ended six weeks after our son, Christopher Michael, was born. Her position was "phased out" while she was on maternity leave. MY INCOME, ALONE, COULD NOT SUSTAIN US! We did not have college degrees, so better paying jobs were not an option!

We tried to sell the house, but the market was slow. On the day of my high school class reunion (June 1987) we had to release the house and return to apartment living. Two months later, money was still so tight that we surrendered the best car. Eventually, we had to move back into my parents' home. We came to grips with living according to our own will and the terribly selfish theme, "It's you and me against the world."

Back on God's Plan
You would have thought that we would have known better, but the enticement to fulfill the American fantasy was really, really strong, especially since we grew up in the inner city where we always had to do without. That was one thing we shared in common and understood very well about one another. For both of us, when we were children, there were so

many winters that the heat or electricity were disconnected that just being able to enjoy these things was a BIG DEAL, now that we were young adults and able to take care of ourselves.

We had begun to acquire a few things and the natural tendency was to gain more. We were able to eat in nice restaurants, buy clothes, and from our perspective, live the dream. We were proud twenty-something year old young people who were homeowners with great jobs.

When it all crashed, we were humbled and had to face the truth about the path that led us to this fall. The truth was that we were no longer focused on God's plans. We had been trying to work our plan while hoping that God would bless it.

Meanwhile, my brother Raphael and his wife Brenda returned to St. Louis to start a church. They began to rally the family to join with them. August of 1987 was the most pivotal period of our lives. It was the month in which Raphael and Brenda Green started Metro Christian Worship Center.

In spite of our continual, massive failures, God was still calling us to step into His plan for Chris and Carol Green. It seemed like terrible timing for us, but God saw it as perfect timing for Him. Over the course of the next 17 years, God totally changed our lives and directed our path to fulfill His purpose.

The precepts and principles of accountability played a major part in our transformation. Since we found ourselves in the ministry, we had to face the battles head on. We could not compromise.

The First Battlefront: Sex
In our journey, the top two battlefronts were sex and money. Let's begin by explaining how our PACT went a long way in helping us to work through issues of sex. Your mate might be battling with strongholds that have been built by years of negative experiences and teaching. When they are feeling insecure in this area, his or her words and actions might not display your definition of insecurity. They may be combative

or clingy. They may be withdrawn or indifferent. Trust us on this one. They are insecure about something.

One of our most precious moments of revelation was during a weekend vacation. We had been married ten years by that time. We went away for a couple of days to rejuvenate and reconnect. After a wonderful romantic encounter the first night, I wanted a repeat performance the next night. However, my wife did not really feel like it, so I got angry. In fact I always got angry when she would say no to sex. I went out onto the balcony of the hotel room and stayed out there for most of the night, sulking.

I was even angrier when I heard her breathing softly inside. She had the nerve to go to sleep! I was furious. I finally trudged back into the room and got into the bed, making sure I stayed on my side of the bed.

The next morning, I was wiped out from the lack of sleep, but I was also still angry. Carol was silent as she showered and dressed. By then, she was irritated because it wasn't like she always said no. This is one of those endless fights that couples go through all the time and we were no different.

The Real Culprit

We still don't know how it happened, but we sat on the bed and I started talking about what happened last night and why this makes me so angry. Remember our PACT was that we would try to stay in a position where we would explain ourselves. The only thing that came to my mind to express my feelings was a memory that suddenly came to me.

I began to tell my wife about an incident in my childhood that I basically had buried until that moment. I recalled, in detail, a seemingly insignificant event from when I was ten years old.

I had been sitting in a musical event that was being conducted in the lower auditorium of the church in which my family attended. Two of my friends were peeking in through a side door and beckoning me to come out and join them. I kept shaking my head because I knew I would get into trouble with my parents if I walked out.

Back in those days, children didn't just walk out of public gatherings. They had to get their parent's permission, even to go to the restroom. The only way to get out was to wait for a transitional moment from one speaker to another or from one choir to another. Then I could sneak out.

Finally such a moment arrived and I jumped up and hurried out to join my partners in some mischief. We ran to the men's restroom, like we had done a hundred times before, but this time, things were different. Just as I entered the restroom, one of them came from behind the door, grabbed my arms and pulled them behind my back while the other one hammered me in my chest with his fists three or four times.

As I recounted the story, I was suddenly overcome with an explosion of emotion that I had held ever since that day. I wailed as I collapsed into Carol's arms, *"They hit me in my chest!"* I convulsed and wept uncontrollably.

The day it actually happened, I never cried. I was physically stronger than the boy who held my arms. I was stronger than both of them, but I was just so devastated by the betrayal that I just stood there and took the blows without resisting the attack.

I had a bad temper as a kid, but I was so dumbfounded that rejection took over instead of my usual violent outburst. I just looked at them while they laughed and laughed. I walked out of the restroom without saying a word and I never said a word to anyone about it until I revealed it all to my wife that day in the hotel.

Suddenly, we understood why I always got angry when my wife said no to sex. We had just pinpointed the day that rejection entered my life. Whenever Carol or anybody turned down requests that were really important to me, it felt like the same blows that I took from those boys in the men's restroom. We realized that I had been wrestling with rejection for most of my life.

Sometimes you may think that you have an anger problem or an anxiety problem, but it is actually a completely different matter altogether. For us, REJECTION was the newly discovered culprit that was messing with our marriage.

During that vacation, Carol handled the situation the way the Bible says wives must deal with husbands when they are unbelievers. Sometimes a Bible toting, scripture quoting, spirit-filled, man of God can behave just like an unbelieving spouse in some area of his life. The principle is the same.

Carol had to trust God and not be afraid. Her biggest fear had been that she would do something that would make me want to leave her. Certainly, a spouse that wants more sex than you do, can cause reasons for fear that he'll leave and pursue someone else. She held steady and saw a breakthrough for her husband.

Deliverance
A couple of years later, the battle in the sexual area was raging again. We don't want to present these stories as if though we gained a victory one time and never had that problem again.

The awareness that rejection was a stronghold was not good enough to defeat the stronghold. That revelation at the hotel only marked the moment that we gained some understanding of what we were facing.

As I mentioned earlier, when I was only three or four years old, I had an encounter with another boy in the neighborhood. Even though I was very young, innocent, naïve and totally not understanding what was going on, it still opened me up to a horrible spirit. I never had any desire to be homosexual, but it opened me up to other sexual lust.

I was officially exposed to pornography in the third grade when I walked up onto a group of boys huddled over a magazine. I saw a naked woman for the first time and something gripped me. I couldn't shake it. In later years, when puberty kicked in, all I knew was that I wanted that feeling. It became a struggle off and on all through high school and college.

I carried it right into the marriage. It was dormant for a long time, but once the internet became available, it was easily accessible and the battle was on for real.

Screen pop ups were constant and sneak peeks started. Instinctively, I'd turn to my wife for relief and that was part of the reason I'd get angry with her for saying no. I'm sure that many times she said no because my approach was primarily out of lust and not love.

I believe a wife knows the difference between when she's being romanced for lovemaking versus pursued for sex. I later learned how important this was when we attended marriage seminars and workshops that featured the male and female circles of contentment that were conducted by Drs. Clarence and Ja'Ola Walker. They gave us insights that strengthened our lives and marriage.

As our public ministry grew, the private battle grew exponentially. Again, since our PACT required being honest with oneself, I got sick and tired of this constant battle in my flesh. I hated being a minister with a secret lust problem.

I knew it was an evil spirit. It was seriously oppressing my life. The night I got delivered, Carol was right there, lying in bed praying for me. She didn't know exactly what it was because I didn't tell her until after I got delivered from it. After hours of restless tossing and turning, I got up out of bed and went straight to my knees. Then I stretched out on the floor and I begged, I mean begged God to deliver me from this. I didn't want this anymore.

As I prayed, I got nauseated. I got physically ill. I got up and ran to our bathroom and threw up. I cannot explain all that happened. I just know that the stronghold left me. I coughed a couple of times and I felt like a ton of weight had come off me. I was light. I was free. The first thing I did was confess to my wife what had been going on with me and what this was really about.

It was from this experience that I wrote one of our most cherished songs titled, "I'm Delivered".

So many years of private frustration
Living under the bondage of religion
Hurting inside when really, I don't know why
But Jesus heard my secret, desperate cry

The shame of lust and pride so deep inside
Will keep me bound, always wondering why
The greater things in God just pass me by
So I yield to Him, surrender all my life

I'm delivered; I'm so grateful just to know
I'm delivered; the Lord has made me whole
I'm delivered; satan has lost control
The Lord restored my soul

It was a victory we shared together. This happened on a Saturday night and the next morning, I confessed to the whole congregation that I had been battling with this lust.

Many people looked at me like I was crazy. I knew I was risking the respect of many people, but I didn't care because I was finally free. I just knew that if this remained in the dark, the enemy of my soul would be able to keep me in the dark. But, if I brought it out into the light, then that evil influence could not remain. We believe that this is the level of transparency you have to be willing to go to with yourself, with your spouse, and with God.

Go and pray for your wife
In the meantime, Carol was dealing with her own sexual issues. There were times when she just didn't feel like sex and it was for no apparent reason at all. We have since learned that many women are in this battle. We had been married about 15 years and we were in the period that was supposed to be the time when a woman's sexual appetite increases.

Even after getting plenty of rest, and there was no children crisis, no job stress, and no emotional or hormonal issues, there was an on-going battle with her just not wanting sex. It became unnatural and not just a physical or emotional thing.

Having since learned to not get so angry when my wife said no, and having been delivered from the strongholds of rejection and lust, my new response was to keep myself busy in ministry affairs: go to the studio, work on music or edit broadcast videos.

After one particular night of futility and frustration, in which we wrestled with the subject of why she didn't feel like having sex, the next morning, I got up and went downstairs to work on some music. For a season, we kept some of the studio equipment in our home. I began playing through some of our tracks and started worshipping. It wasn't long before the tears began to stream down my face as I fully engaged in singing to the Lord.

Outside of the room, I heard Carol come downstairs and go into our laundry room. At that very instant, the Spirit of God spoke in my heart and said, *"Go pray for your wife."*

Suddenly, the tears stopped, the warm fuzzy feeling departed, and I was left with nothing but a command. I tried to keep singing and worshipping, but all the glory and splendor of the moment was gone. All that remained was those words, *"Go pray for your wife."*

I didn't want to go and pray for her. From my perspective, I was right and she was wrong. I had chosen the right response by going away to pray and worship. I thought I was being spiritual and she was carnal. I felt righteous and justified. Now there was silence.

The Spirit of God wasn't saying anything. Why? Well, because I had responded in pride. This was not about love in any way. If I loved my wife, I would be trying to find out why this was happening to her.

I turned off the music and slowly made my way to the laundry room to face her. She was very frustrated about the matter, too. I walked up to her and said, *"The Lord told me to come pray for you."*

She just looked at me as if to say, *"O, He did?"*

It was an extremely awkward moment, but I put my hand on her shoulder and began to pray. We had been taught to pray in the Spirit and wait for the Lord to give us what to say, so I did that.

God gives me pictures in my mind when I pray. I saw that an evil spirit came against the women in Carol's family to take away their sexual desire, so that their husbands would be easily tempted to stray away into adultery. I began to realize that this was a multi-generational spirit that had come through her family line to destroy our marriage. I spoke out what I saw and my wife just broke down and cried.

Afterwards, Carol admitted that she had been just as frustrated as me. She said she had been trying to get a handle on this for years. This gave us greater insight as to why so much had gone wrong in her family.

This was one of the incidents that helped us to see how vital it is for a husband to take the lead in guarding and protecting his wife and children. Husbands have been given authority to pull down strongholds in their own homes.

While a lot of Christian ministers are clamoring to be in the spotlight, displaying spiritual power, we learned that this was where it really counted. Can you stand in a laundry room and tear down a multi-generational curse that is plaguing your wife? Can you sit in a hotel room or your own bedroom and help your husband press through to an emotional and spiritual breakthrough?

We also came to realize that part of our sexual battles were the result of crossing boundaries before we got married. We opened the door for the enemy to come in and attack us in this area. By being open and honest about it with each other and the Lord, we saw great breakthrough in our union.

We have living proof: The accountability factor led us to deliverance and healing in our sex life.

Our PACT and money

The other major area of battle was in our finances. This fight was not so much a war being waged BETWEEN us as much as it was a war AGAINST us.

Since we both dropped out of college, we had put ourselves in a very difficult economic position. We had set a course where we would have to take the minimum wage jobs and work our way up the ladder within a company. We were not discounting the grace and favor that God could give us for promotion and advancement. We just had to be real about taking entry-level positions.

Even in the Bible, we saw how God powerfully used educated, trained and prepared people in higher levels of society. Yes, God also used uneducated folks to speak to and preach to high society and rich people, but rarely did those people advance and enter into that world as part of their lifestyle.

We couldn't complain about it. We had made the decisions and we had to deal with it for many, many years. God blessed us through the years to obtain some pretty good jobs with decent income. Who knows; maybe high school diplomas carried people a lot further back in those years. We can honestly say that we were prepared for the workforce of that era.

I handled our monthly budget and right from the beginning of our marriage, we opened a joint bank account. In fact, we have always, always, always had a joint bank account. We feel that if you can't trust a person enough to share your bank account, then you probably shouldn't marry them.

We had our money disagreements just like any other couple. One of the biggest conflicts was about all the various female necessities. Before I got married, I had never known that it was possible to run out of toilet paper in less than a month. Then there were the hair products, lotions, creams, O' my God, where does it all end?

I was not feeling it and I structured the finances like a military commander. Even though it was a joint account, I dictated the priorities and expenditures. Remember, I could not handle the stress of unexpected expenses, so I controlled the checkbook out of absolute fear.

For many years, Carol did the best she could with what I allotted, but we basically spent the money on food, bills, and my occasional whims to buy electronic gadgets whenever I got depressed and stressed out about my job or some other issue in life that I couldn't handle.

You're right, that wasn't fair, yet many who control the finances, whether it's the husband or the wife, are guilty of this. We force our spouse to make-do with what's in the budget, but we will cross the lines with our own secret impulse purchases.

No seed, no harvest
During our fantasy chase, we fell into the trap where we stopped sowing and giving to the church. In fact, we stopped attending church for weeks at a time. After our world caved in, we never had enough money. We failed to realize that the reason we didn't have enough money was because we didn't plant any seeds. It's a wicked cycle and the only way to get out of it was to start giving again. It's like a basic law of nature. You cannot expect to reap a crop if you never sow any seeds.

As a kid growing up in church I heard Matthew 6:33 all the time: *"Therefore do not worry, saying, 'What shall we eat?' or 'What shall we drink?' or 'What shall we wear?' For after all these things the Gentiles seek. For your heavenly Father knows that you need all these things. But seek first the kingdom of God and His righteousness, and all these things shall be added to you".* (Matthew 6:31-33, NKJV)

We were faced with the choice to live by this Biblical principle or continue to live by the madness of chasing fantasies. God was telling us to stop pursuing money. If we kept chasing money, we would never get our needs met.

We were going to have to practice what we would someday preach. We realized that accepting our new roles to help establish a new church meant that we needed be consistent in church attendance and giving. That was the first step in getting back on track. We started slowly by just donating what we could until we were able to build up to a consistent giving level. We also had to become more responsible in managing our personal finances. Committing to these two practices started us on a slow, but steady process to financial recovery.

My Daughter, Your Wife
Several years into our financial recovery process, God got my attention when he blessed Carol in a very powerful way. One of the women in our local church was a self-employed professional beautician with her own facility. She offered my wife free weekly hair care, for an entire year.

In the midst of celebrating this blessing, God spoke to me and said, *"I wanted you to know how important my daughter is to me, so I did this for her. When this year of free hair care is over, you are to set your wife's needs in the family budget."*

That's exactly what I did. I started making adjustments in my spending habits, so that I would be prepared for the change. We kept our joint bank account, but we opened a separate bank account, just for Carol, to take care of her needs. Since we were honoring God with our financial giving, we were observing increases in income and decreases in expense. By the time that period of free hair care ended, I was able to set aside an allowance for my wife and that practice continues to this day.

Even when we hit difficult financial seasons, I still transferred funds into her allowance account. Many times, she would sacrifice her allowance to help in hard times, but that decision was hers to make. I didn't dictate it. I transferred the money and she would help pay bills out of her personal account, if that became necessary. The point was that I still obeyed God and honored her.

The PACT and Prosperity
Over the span of several years of restoration, we progressed from renting apartments to renting a home. We were such

faithful and good paying tenants of that home that our landlord offered us the opportunity to move into and takeover the payments on their residence, which was a huge house in a great part of town. God blessed us to return to home ownership.

We financed a pre-owned Audi and paid it off. Then we financed our first brand new vehicle, a conversion van. We consulted a financial advisor who showed us how to consolidate our debt and establish a savings account. Following his advice, we accomplished our goal of having only one monthly payment and that was the mortgage. We had no consumer debt. Like prior years, we drove two vehicles, but this time we paid off both of them. We had no balances on our credit cards. If we used them, we would pay off the balance by the end of the month.

We also noticed an amazing thing happened after we built up our savings account. We kept at least $1000 in the account and suddenly we didn't have any emergencies: no car repairs, no major home repairs, no unexpected medical events; it all stopped as soon as we established and maintained the savings account. We learned that having a mote built around our castle (as our financial consultant called it) took away any demonic ability to keep our finances in a tailspin. It took away those evil opportunities to keep our lives in financial chaos. We experienced the peace of a settled household.

God didn't always use money to bless us. Many times, HE simply met the need. When our twin sons, Jonathan Mark and David Matthew were born, we did not have medical insurance, and due to some prenatal complications, Carol was in and out of the hospital several times. The medical bill came to $32,000. When we called to make payment arrangements, the bill was miraculously reduced to $300.

People began to give us things. Our children wore the latest designer clothes and we never bought them. They wore the latest shoes and we never spent our money to obtain them. Our refrigerator was always full of food. We began to testify to others, *"You don't need money, all you need is God."*

We were so free financially that we opened another bank account and called it our 'Giving' account. We set aside 15 to 20 percent of our monthly income into this account so that we could give more to our local church, other ministries, and individuals who needed assistance.

And, yes, it all began when we acted upon this important part of the PACT, the place of making ourselves accountable to one another. Don't get the wrong idea. This was not an instant turn around. This was a very long, fourteen-year process, but it was worth every minute, hour, day, week, month and year. By the time God launched us forth into our own ministry in another city, we were financially sound enough to make that step.

Benefits or Consequences

Having shared these stories, we still must keep our message balanced because we have some difficult matters to discuss regarding choices. None of our success would have been possible if either of us had not chosen to walk together.

Going back to Peter's instructions in dealing with an unbelieving spouse; if a Godly husband or wife obeys the teachings of the Bible, it does not mean that their obedience will have some mystical sway on their spouse's heart and cause him or her to fall in step with the ways of God. They still have the power to choose.

Wives, likewise, be submissive to your own husbands, that even if some do not obey the word, they, without a word, may be won by the conduct of their wives, when they observe your chaste conduct accompanied by fear. (1 Peter 3: 1-2, NKJV)

Peter's instructions were never meant to be used like magical words of witchcraft to cast a spell on your spouse and change their behavior. With every scripture from the Bible, people can make a choice. God doesn't force people to come to Him or stay with Him. He gives everyone a choice. He even gives us a choice in our response if our spouse is unfaithful and leaves.

Some preachers have used 1 Corinthians 7:14 to say that the wife's faith guarantees the salvation of her husband because it reads: *For the unbelieving husband is made holy because of his wife, and the unbelieving wife is made holy because of her husband. Otherwise your children would be unclean, but as it is, they are holy.*

This scripture is referring to how God acknowledges and honors their marriage and the children because of the believing spouse. This does not mean that God considers the unbelieving spouse holy as it relates to a righteous standing in God. He considers the marriage holy.

Any spouse, in their rebellion, may choose to sever the relationship simply because he/she does not want to follow Christ. The important thing is that you cannot allow that fear and threat to convert you into an agent of manipulation, intimidation or domination.

Just remember, with choices come benefits or consequences. For instance, there are consequences for an offending husband's decisions and one of them is that his prayers will be hindered. God won't hear and answer his prayers until he gets things right with his wife.

*In the same way you married men should live considerately with [your wives], with an intelligent recognition [of the marriage relation], honoring the woman as [physically] the weaker, but [realizing that you] are joint heirs of the grace (God's unmerited favor) of life, **in order that your prayers may not be hindered and cut off***. (1 Peter 3:7, Amplified)

You still have to trust God for grace and wisdom that will carry you through the situation, no matter how your mate responds to God or to you. Never use the Word of God to manipulate your spouse. That's not what accountability is about. Remember it's about YOU staying in the position to be explainable to them; not making sure you keep THEM in a position to be answerable to you.

Marriage Isn't 50-50
Quite often we have heard some celebrity explaining their marital relationship by saying marriage is 50-50. That sounds like a nice sound-byte and it makes a clever quote on a

Facebook status, but it's not reality. Dr. Dennis Rainey explains it best that 50-50 doesn't work in marriage.

First of all, you cannot determine if your spouse has met you half way. What, exactly, is half way? Your spouse may feel like they are giving their all to the marriage, but you might determine their effort as being mediocre at best.

Secondly, the 50-50 arrangements make you focus on what you think your spouse is NOT doing. It makes you focus on their weaknesses and faults. It makes you feel that you are doing most of the work.

Thirdly, we believe that marriage is actually about giving whatever you have, and receiving whatever your spouse has to offer. You must learn to appreciate where they are and what they have without trying to determine if it meets your personal standards. Sometimes marriage is 90-10, 100-0, 75-25, 60-40, or even 20-20 because neither of you can do enough to make the relationship work.

Perfect Love to Imperfect People
Godly marriage is about the perfect love that Jesus taught about in Matthew 5:48. *"Be ye perfect as your father in heaven is perfect."*

When Jesus made this statement it was spoken in the context of Matthew 5:44, *"But I say unto you, Love your enemies, bless them that curse you, do good to them that hate you, and pray for them which despitefully use you, and persecute you."*

In this context, the word perfect was referring to unconditional love. Jesus Christ was telling His followers to love people without reservation, to love without qualification, to love unconditionally. Therefore *'be perfect like your Father in heaven is perfect'* was not talking about flawless living. He was telling us to love people the same way God loves people, which is perfectly. It's about perfect love to imperfect people.

There is no fear in love; but perfect love casts out fear, because fear involves torment. But he who fears has not been made perfect in love. (1 John 4:18, NKJV)

We're certainly not referring to your mate as your enemy, but the principle of love is the same. That's why *perfect love cast out fear.*

If you love your spouse without holding anything back, without waiting for them to earn it, and without setting up conditions in your mind that they must meet, then the Word of God promises that their fears will be driven out. You will become an extension of God's healing hand to their heart.

One of the most valuable nuggets we gained was that we had to distinguish the difference between something that was actually wrong versus something that we just didn't like about the other person. No one should have to change simply because of our personal preferences. Change should be the result of uncovering something that will be harmful to them or the relationship, not just a pet peeve.

This understanding also helped us in raising our children, so that we wouldn't exasperate them by forcing them to conform to our personal likes and dislikes.

We learned that a lot of our negative reactions to one another were rooted in fear, but the perfect love of God, being poured out through each of us, literally drove out our fears. It drove out the fear that he will leave me. It drove out the fear that she will find someone else. It drove out the fear of failure.

Resist the negative thoughts and past experiences that are telling you that this is just a bunch of fairy tale rhetoric. The resistance goes something like this, *"That may have worked for Chris and Carol and a few other people, but I live in the urban world, in the real world. There are no men or women like that here."*

We are shouting it out to you, ""That's a lie from satan!"

In John 10:10 Jesus declared, *"The thief does not come except to steal, and to kill, and to destroy. I have come that they may have life, and that they may have it more abundantly."*

We are talking about the abundant life for marriage.

Agreement and Attitude
We learned that the blessings that we desired for our relationship were connected to two ingredients within the accountability factor: Agreement and Attitude.

Did you know that a couple doesn't have to ask God to bless them if they just come together in agreement? That's the place where God commands the blessing over them.

"Behold, how good and how pleasant it is for brethren to dwell together in unity.... For there the LORD commanded the blessing— Life forevermore." (Psalm 133:1 and 3b, NKJV)

When a couple comes into agreement with one another and with God, they become ten times more effective. A question is asked in Deuteronomy 32:30, *How could one chase a thousand, And two put ten thousand to flight, unless their Rock had sold them, and the LORD had surrendered them?*

With a combination of our unity and the Lord fighting on our behalf, we can become ten times stronger and unstoppable. We know this may sound like religious babble and a lot of deep spiritual talk that isn't based in reality. It will feel like that, until you make a change in your attitude about what God desires to do in your life.

You were taught, with regard to your former way of life, to put off your old self, which is being corrupted by its deceitful desires; to be made new in the attitude of your minds; (Ephesians 4:22-23, NKJV)

You have to change your attitude if you want to see a change in your relationships. The most effective way to change your attitude is to renew your mind through the Word of God.

And do not be conformed to this world, but be transformed by the renewing of your mind, that you may prove what is that good and acceptable and perfect will of God.
(Romans 12:2, NKJV)

This means that you not only have to change WHAT you think, but you must change the WAY you think. That's the kind of change that requires a transformation. The meaning of the word *transformed* in this scripture describes the kind of change a caterpillar goes through to become a butterfly.

Right now, you might be emotionally crawling along through life, barely able to cover any distance after days or weeks of labor. But after the transformation, you will be able to fly and cover the same distance in a matter of seconds.

That's how radical the change will be if you stop conforming to this society's view of relationships and allow the Word of God to change you completely. This change is necessary in order to receive and understand this revelation about accountability.

Hey, we're just telling you what happened to us. We know it will happen with you. We feel like one of those couples that you may have seen on the TV infomercials, trying to convince people to try out some special product that worked for them.

Well, our product is the **Word of God**, brought to you by the **Spirit of God**, all under the orchestration and executive plan of **Father God**. Just try it! It will change your life!

Accountability was the precept that literally saved our marriage. We encourage you to give serious consideration to this part of the PACT.

If you are reading this book with your spouse or fiancée, just turn to them right now and speak these words. If you are unmarried speak them to God:

"I promise to keep myself in the position where I will be answerable, explainable and accountable to you."

Commitment

Commitment to God

The commitment within our PACT did not begin with Chris' commitment to Carol or Carol's commitment to Chris. It actually began with God's commitment to Chris and Carol. God's commitment to us triggered our response of commitment to Him and to one another.

Before we talk about the commitment that a husband and wife need to make to one another, we must talk about the commitment that God has made to all of us. In fact, the commitment of all Christian Believers can be attributed to a revelation of and response to God's love. There is nothing like coming face to face with the genuine unconditional love of God. In Romans 5:8 the Bible declares, *"But God demonstrates His own love toward us, in that while we were still sinners, Christ died for us."*

One of the failures in Christian marriage is due to two human beings trying to deal with one another without understanding why God brought them together. They don't realize that He plans to use each of them to facilitate the other's healing. But first, many need to learn what the Lord has already done on their behalf.

When we acknowledge and appreciate what God has done for us, it makes our hearts open, grateful, humble and capable of loving others (our spouse in particular) the way God loves us. That's what gives us the ability to extend mercy, unconditional love and respect to one another. It gives us the ability to see beyond our own needs and to see theirs.

As we talk about the commitment aspect of the PACT, we want to deal with it at three levels: Commitment to People, Commitment to Process and Commitment to Purpose.

Commitment to People

As we behold the heart of God the Father, we can see that He is committed first and foremost to people. Each person matters to God. We can see His commitment through the parables that Jesus told to help us understand His Father.

In Luke 15, Jesus tells stories about a lost sheep, a lost coin and a lost son. Each story is meant to help us understand how valuable each person is to God. If a shepherd can leave 99 sheep in the fold and go searching for the missing one, this defies earthly logic. Since he had 99% of the sheep accounted for, why take the risk and go after the missing one? Answer: Every sheep matters; none are expendable.

When a woman lost one coin from her necklace of ten, she tears the house apart trying to find it. Historical customs reveal that the coin is so valuable because the entire necklace is a wedding gift. Every coin matters, none are expendable.

A wasteful son demands his inheritance, thus declaring his father to be dead to him, and leaves home. The father is so glad when he returns that he restores everything back to him including his status and inheritance. Against the protest of his elder son, the father declares that his younger son, who was lost, is now found. Both sons matter; neither was expendable.

These stories reveal God's commitment to people. This revelation not only invokes gratitude, but it should inspire grace and mercy in us for others, namely our spouse.

The Bible describes the relationship between a husband and a wife like that of Christ and the church. If you had a bad marriage or your parents divorced, it can be very hard to relate to God in this way. Unfortunately, since a lot of teaching and preaching is focused upon faultfinding and sin searching, many people find it difficult to see a relationship with God in a healthy way.

When pastors teach that God will kick people out of His family at the slightest error and mistake, then they're telling me that I have more love for my wife than God has for me. I cannot accept that teaching. I made my wife a promise even before we got married. I told her that I would never leave her. Then I set out to prove it.

I believe that's the way we are loved by God. Once we give our hearts and lives to Him, we become a part of the church and we become His bride. HE promised to never leave us and

HE set out to prove it. We may wander away like a sheep, get lost like a coin, or runaway like a rebellious son, but God never gives up on us. No one is expendable.

Even though we may be struggling in some areas of our lives, our blemishes, spots and wrinkles do not turn GOD away. Many have misquoted a particular scripture in the Bible and said Jesus is coming for a church without blemishes, spots and wrinkles, but read it for your self. That's not what the Bible says.

"Husbands, love your wives, just as Christ also loved the church and gave Himself for her, that He might sanctify and cleanse her with the washing of water by the word, that He might present her to Himself a glorious church, not having spot or wrinkle or any such thing, but that she should be holy and without blemish. So husbands ought to love their own wives as their own bodies; he who loves his wife loves himself." (Ephesians 5: 25-28, NKJV)

The writer says that God will **present to Himself** a church (bride) that will be without spots or wrinkles. We understand this to mean that He's going to clean and prepare the church Himself, for Himself. And HE's going to do it by the washing of water that comes through His Word. HE's going to do it in a patient, loving way.

Just so that you understand us clearly, this scripture was written in the context of **how husbands are to love their wives**. So a husband is NOT being told to let his wife get herself prepared for him and if she's not perfect, then the husband has the right to reject her.

No, the writer was telling husbands to love their wives the same way Christ loves the church; which is unconditional acceptance of who she really is right now, and total commitment to help her become all that she is meant to be.

Commitment to Process
This understanding carries over to the next part of our discussion on commitment: God is committed to process.

There is a process that we go through to reach maturity and wholeness. God is totally committed to do whatever it takes to see us through that process.

Lifting Branches

Again, we're going to be a little controversial as we make this point about our process in God.

"I am the true vine, and My Father is the vinedresser. Every branch in Me that does not bear fruit He takes away; and every branch that bears fruit He prunes, that it may bear more fruit." (John 15: 1-2, NKJV)

Many preachers and teachers quote this scripture in such a way that it portrays God as an intolerant being who has no compassion for His people's growth process. We have been taught that anyone who does not bear fruit is cut off.

In our study of this scripture, we learned that the meaning of the Greek word for **takes away** has four definitions. Three of the four definitions mean **'to lift up'** and one of those three means to lift up in order to carry. Only the fourth definition means to remove, and even that removal is talking about what is removed FROM the branch, NOT the removal OF the branch itself.

These four definitions describe the actual practice of what takes place when a vinedresser has nonproductive or under productive branches on their vines. The more accurate meaning would be: Any branch that is not producing fruit, the vinedresser lifts it from its current position on the trellis and trains it to grow in a different position, where it can become fruitful.

One of the reasons this is done is so that branches that are not receiving enough sunlight or sap flow can be moved to spots where they are able to receive it. There is also a season of removing shoots, leaves and unproductive sections from the branch to help it to become fruitful.

Many preachers and teachers have been misinterpreting the removal aspect and not understood the entire vine dressing process. Historically, vine dressers in Biblical times, spent a lot of time lifting and moving branches on the trellis. They did not instantly cut off unfruitful branches. They would give new and young vines a season or two, to become productive.

Can you see the lengths that God is willing go to in helping you through your process? That's why God might be moving you to a different church assembly, different job, or different community. You may have become unfruitful in your current status, so HE is shifting you. He's simply moving you to a different position on the trellis where you can receive the radiant light of His Word; from which you can finally become fruitful. He didn't cut you off the vine because HE knew you were in a position where you were not able to bear fruit. In this season of your life, HE is lifting you, just like a vine dresser.

Now that you are in a different position and environment, don't get discouraged and don't give up. Yes, we know what that feels like, too. It is uncomfortable and nothing is like what you are accustomed to, but you are in the process of God. He is committed to seeing you through the process. He is committed to rebuilding, restoring and renewing your heart, home and marriage.

Qualifications for Casting Out
We can just hear some of you who grew up in church asking a ton of questions. Chris and Carol, how dare you say that God doesn't cut off unfruitful Believers! It's right there in the Bible.

*"I am the vine, you are the branches. He who abides in Me, and I in him, bears much fruit; for without Me you can do nothing. **If anyone does not abide in Me**, he is cast out as a branch and is withered; and they gather them and throw them into the fire, and they are burned."* (John 15: 5-6, NKJV)

Well, according to this passage only a person **who does not abide in the vine** is cast out as a branch that is withered. Unfruitfulness does not cause the casting out. Failure to abide in the vine causes the casting out.

People are unfruitful for many reasons, including just plain old lack of teaching in their homes and churches. Please don't tell us that you think God is casting out Believers when they are in a situation of such poor teaching that it is causing them to be unfruitful.

In other cases, people are in a season of loss or grief and they are unfruitful. Please don't tell us that you feel they will be cast out while they are grieving or in depression.

We really have to be careful what family philosophies and lifeless sermons we repeat without really looking at the Bible ourselves and thinking about what we are communicating. A more mature understanding would be: Anyone who fails to abide in the vine is unfruitful. Not everyone who is unfruitful has failed to abide in the vine.

Why Did Jesus Curse the Fig Tree?
Still someone is asking, *"What about the unfruitful fig tree that Jesus cursed in Mark 11?"* Our response is that the cursing of the fig tree was a lesson on FAITH, not a statement about unfruitful Believers being cursed, cut off, or cast into hell. Let's look at it:

*Now in the morning, as they passed by, they saw the fig tree dried up from the root. And Peter, remembering, said to Him, "Rabbi, look! The fig tree which You cursed has withered away." So Jesus answered and said to them, "**Have faith in God**. For assuredly, I say to you, whoever says to this mountain, 'Be removed and be cast into the sea,' and does not doubt in his heart, but believes that those things he says will be done, he will have whatever he says. Therefore I say to you, whatever things you ask when you pray, believe that you receive them, and you will have them.* (Mark 11: 20-24, NKJV)

The cursing of the fig tree was an object lesson. If Jesus' point had been that the tree represented unfruitful Believers and that God curses unfruitfulness, He would have said that.

Instead, His response to Peter gives us the true purpose of the event. He informs them that just like HE was able to speak to the fig tree, WE can speak to a mountain. Then He told them what would happen if they pray in faith. The entire passage was a faith lesson. It had nothing to do with unfruitful Believers.

We're emphasizing this so strongly because we want you to get free from religious bondage and doctrine. GOD IS COMMITED TO TAKING YOU THROUGH THE PROCESS TO MAKE YOU FRUITFUL. He's not looking for any and every little reason to cut you off, cut you down, or cast you away. All of that other stuff is religion and man's doctrine. It is not the heart of God toward you, your mate or your children.

Let it grow, let it grow, let it grow
You can also see God's commitment to process in the parable about the wheat and the tares:

*Another parable He put forth to them, saying: "The kingdom of heaven is like a man who sowed good seed in his field; but while men slept, his enemy came and sowed tares among the wheat and went his way. But when the grain had sprouted and produced a crop, then the tares also appeared. So the servants of the owner came and said to him, 'Sir, did you not sow good seed in your field? How then does it have tares?' He said to them, 'An enemy has done this.' The servants said to him, 'Do you want us then to go and gather them up?' But he said, 'No, lest while you gather up the tares you also uproot the wheat with them. **Let both grow together until the harvest**, and at the time of harvest I will say to the reapers, "First gather together the tares and bind them in bundles to burn them, but gather the wheat into my barn."*
(Matthew 13: 24-30 NKJV)

From this parable we learn three important lessons:
• God is so confident of the success of His seed that He's not worried about what the enemy had sown into His field.
• God allows the wicked to grow side by side with what He has sown. He's not concerned about it growing together.
• We should not waste time and energy trying to get rid of the weeds that are growing around us. God will deal with it.

Isn't it awesome to see the level of God's commitment to take you through your process, so that you can reach maturity and fruitfulness in your life and relationships? Even weeds sown around us cannot stop us from growing. With this kind of commitment from the Lord, we are enlightened, encouraged and empowered to commit to Him in a fresh way.

Many years ago, we wrote a special song that expresses this kind of commitment to God. The lyrics are:

I will continue with Jesus in the garden of decision.
Continue with Him when I'm running endless miles.
Continue with Jesus through the times of tribulation.
Continue with Him through this trial.
Continue with Him through it all.

Committed to Purpose

God is committed to people. God is committed to process. God is also committed to purpose. What is God's purpose for your marriage? Why did you get married? Why did you marry that particular person?

People get married for all kinds of reasons: Sex, money, escape from parental control or from an abusive home situation, affluence, influence, status, peer pressure, parent pressure, and a long list of personal, cultural and social purposes.

Did you know that God has a purpose for marriage? Dr. Dennis Rainey explains God's purpose for marriage in his teaching on Achieving Oneness in Marriage. He lists five reasons for marriage, which are to:

MIRROR God's image
MULTIPLY a Godly heritage
MANAGE God's realm
MUTUALLY complete one another
MODEL Christ's relationship to the church

We strongly encourage you to include this teaching in your personal library. Once you understand what God had in mind for your marriage, it solidifies your understanding of what God is seeking to do through your marriage.

Purpose for Marriage

When it is understood that God is committed to purpose, a couple develops the intestinal fortitude to stand against the storms of life. Most of what we have talked about has had to do with the internal battles in a relationship. So far we haven't talked very much about the other side of a two edged sword: dealing with the opposition from outside forces.

We believe that a marriage must also be fortified to deal with the storms that come from the outside. One of the key factors that helped us face these kind of storms was the knowledge that God had a purpose for our relationship.

Strength and Courage

Purpose really made us strong. Looking back, we are amazed at the tenacity and strength that was forged inside of us to withstand all kinds of wiles, schemes and attacks.

Yes, even temptation to commit adultery came our way, but it was absolutely squashed because the purpose of God was far more valuable than a temporary thrill.

A young lady asked me to take her home after one midweek service. She waited around until almost everyone was gone and requested a ride home. This was at the same time we were having a hard time in our marriage. Our children were very young and life was hectic. We didn't have time to talk like we used to and sex was not happening at all. Although this young lady was pretty, too much Godly purpose had been built into the fiber of our marriage.

I opened an office in the lobby area of the church and told her that she could use the telephone to call someone to come and take her home. Then I went to my office, located on the other side of the building, on the second floor. Temptation smashed!

As we mentioned earlier, before our twins were born, Carol was constantly in and out of the hospital. This was a very difficult pregnancy as she threatened premature birth in her sixth month.

During one of her routine hospital visits, things got really serious and they needed to keep her overnight. I decided to stay in the room with her. I just felt like something was wrong. There was a tense feeling within me throughout the entire night. I felt that if I stopped praying, I would lose her and the babies. As I prayed, in my spirit I saw my wife lying in the bed with a bright light shining on her, but just outside of the light, darkness was trying to close in. I wrestled all night with that image in my mind.

The Spirit of God kept repeating one scripture to me over and over again, *"Be strong and of good courage!"* from Joshua 1:9. The entire passage actually reads: *Have I not commanded you? Be strong and of good courage; do not be afraid, nor be dismayed, for the LORD your God is with you wherever you go.*

The next morning, Carol overheard her doctor reprimanding the night shift doctor for having her medication dosage too high. The mistake could have had very serious consequences.

The LORD'S plans stand firm forever; his intentions can never be shaken. (Psalm 33:11, NLTV)

Looking back at that night, which we will never forget the rest of our lives, we see that it was the purpose of God that carried us through it. His purpose was stronger than the threat of death. God was so committed to His purpose for our marriage that He moved on me in intercession. God's purpose for our marriage saved us from becoming the victims of a medical malpractice. When we say that God is committed to purpose, we are not being theological or theoretical. We have lived it.

We realize there are people who prayed for loved ones who died anyway. We cannot provide an answer as to why that happened. We can only tell you what happened in our situations. All we know is that His word declares:

You can make many plans, but the LORD'S purpose will prevail. (Proverbs 19:21, NLTV)

Commitment to One Another

Since we are in covenant with the God of the universe who has committed Himself to us, our process and our purpose, how could we dare withhold our commitment to Him and to one another as husband and wife?

Only from this foundation of God's commitment to people, process and purpose, can we talk about the commitment a husband and wife must make to one another. Now we can talk about how God's commitment is what empowers us to love Him and one another.

The PACT involved a commitment that went beyond our emotions. It was a DESCION to commit to one another. It was a decision to commit to one another's process. It was a decision to commit to one another's purpose.

Eventually, this commitment opened our eyes to see that even though my family was crushed by death and Carol's family was shattered by divorce, God had brought us together to demonstrate and declare that there could be life after loss, joy after tears, hope after disappointment and purpose could come out of pain.

Please take a serious look at the **Commitment** part of the PACT. Commitment has literally preserved our marriage. We encourage you to give genuine consideration to this part of the PACT, too.

If you are reading this book with your spouse or fiancée, just turn to them right now and speak these words. If you are unmarried speak them to God:

"I promise to commit to you. I promise to commit to your process. I promise to commit to your purpose."

Trust

The Fight

Trust was not so much a principle that we learned, as it was the result of making and sticking to our promise. Trust was established over time. It can be as strong as the bridge that holds the weight of vehicles and at the same time, be as fragile and delicate as the petals on a flower. Just when you feel your relationship can conquer anything in the world, you find yourself in the middle of another disagreement and wondering how you're going to get through this one.

Even as 20-year veterans, conducting pre-marital classes and modeling faithfulness before a new crop of young people who were attending our church, we still found ourselves bickering and fighting, from time to time, over things that touched those sensitive parts of our hearts.

While on the way to attend the wedding of one of the couples that completed our pre-marital class, we got into a whale of an argument. We hadn't had a conflict like this one in years. I let out a couple of sarcastic words to make my point and Carol, who had long ago lost her fear to engage, was sending her shots right back at me. The scrapping was over an on-going issue of balancing priorities between the ministry and our family.

Earlier that week, I was late picking her up from an appointment because I had some ministry responsibilities to complete. We had a short curt conversation, but it was far from over. It spilled over to the morning we were hurriedly getting dressed to attend the wedding. The frustration had been mounting all week and both pots were boiling. We went back and forth so long that we missed the wedding because we were sitting in our vehicle arguing. We still had time to make it to the reception, so we drove to that location instead. When we arrived, we were still going at it until Carol finally said, *"Just take me home!"*

Man, in all our years, she had never responded like that. I knew I had hurt her feelings and I didn't mean to do that. I was just trying to get her to see my position. We drove home in silence. After we got home, the entire day was just awkward. Our sons knew something was wrong and the whole household was quiet. It was that way for about eight hours.

Somewhere between 11:00 and midnight, I went into the bedroom to make one more attempt to settle this. I sat down on the bed with Carol positioned on the complete opposite side. Sister girl was still fuming, man. I didn't know where to start or what to say, but what came out was pure Godly inspiration.

"Dear," I said *"I want to lose this fight."*

I watched her shoulders deflate like a balloon going down.

"I need to say what I need to say, but I need you to tell me if what I'm seeing and what I'm thinking is what's really happening. I'm not accusing you of anything. I just need to be able to express my thoughts and you can tell me what it is from your perspective."

Needless to say, we talked all night. That breakthrough was the result of TRUST. Years and years of accountability and commitment had led our relationship to a place where even our disagreements could be resolved without it being about who was right and who was wrong. It was an evolution in our marriage.

Truth and Transparency
Trust in marriage is connected with two key elements: truth and transparency. In that particular disagreement, there had been several thoughts that had been plaguing us about what should be our priorities in given situations. Carol felt I was placing the ministry ahead of her and the family. I felt that she needed to view the ministry as my job and not "just the ministry." We both had valid points. However, it was not about whose point of view was the right one. This was a matter of looking at the same thing from different angles.

It was like looking at some object on a table from opposite sides. From my side, the object is red. From Carol's side, the object is blue. We were both right, because we didn't know that we were looking at a two-colored object. We had to stop, come over to the other's side of the table, and see that we we're both correct in what we observed, but both wrong in our conclusions.

Many times we associate right and wrong with truth. We can hold on to our point of view with all our might and fail to recognize that even though we are correct about what we see, **we don't know the truth** about what we see.

If a couple is still battling over accountability and commitment issues, they can never reach the necessary levels of trust that it will take to get past conflicts that require complete transparency.

Vulnerability is another way of describing transparency. God gave me profound words to express my desire for us to get past that very strong conflict. It was more important that our relationship was right, than for ME to be right. So the only way to break past the stalemate was to let go of my desire to be right. The wisdom to express this all came out as a simple anger defusing statement, *"I want to lose this fight."*

Are you willing to lose an argument so that you can get to the truth? We discovered that there had been years and years of unresolved conflicts simply because of incidents, observations and statements that were swayed by our points of view and not from a position of truth.

We talked almost all night because we found ourselves on a journey back through the years of many conflicts in which we had been looking at the same thing, but coming to the wrong conclusions.

One of the definitions of the word truth is **reality**. We often believe that truth is a set of facts and figures that can be easily observed. We will stake our reputation on the facts and the stats. Bishop Raphael Green often makes this quote, *"Liars can figure and figures can lie."*

As pastors, we have encountered people who are upset with the happenings within a church because they feel the leaders won't tell the truth about what's going on in the lives of people in their congregation. However, there's more to being truthful than just exposing the secret sins and faults of people. It may be a fact that many people go to the nightclubs, drink and come to church hung-over. However, the truth (reality) could be that they keep coming to church because they're looking for someone to help them.

Please don't be religious and judgmental with your spouse. Keep it real and stay vulnerable to them. Keep your heart open to their point of view. Your way of seeing the world is not the only view. You will discover that their point of view is just as real to them as yours is to you. You will discover that their point of view is not wrong; you've never stepped over to their side of the table.

Faults
Throughout this book we have mentioned my brother Mark Green. He was three years older than me and quite a character. He died in October of 1999 due to AIDS related complications. Even though he was married to a great woman and had two outstanding children, he had a secret and an inner struggle that he was not able to expose to family and friends until it was too late.

We learned a lot about ourselves through Mark's life and death and one of those lessons had to do with having enough trust in one another to confess our real pain.

The Bible says that we are to confess our faults:

Confess your faults one to another, and pray one for another, that ye may be healed. The effectual fervent prayer of a righteous man availeth much. (James 5:16, KJV)

The word fault does not simply mean guilt or wrong doings. A fault is also a place where you are fragile, cracked, broken and pressured to the point where you snap. The expression of that break usually comes out in some sin, habit, vice or behavior.

The Bible is actually telling us to confess our broken places; confess our fragile places; confess our pain. From a geological point of view, a fault is a crack created by stress in the earth's crust. We have always thought of a person's faults as just simply being their sins, habits, vices or behavior.

God opened our understanding to see every person's heart and life like the earth, which has stress points that break under pressure. The spot where the break occurs is called a fault. When the break occurs it is called an earthquake.

We learned that there are at least three types of stress on the earth's crust. They are tension, compression and shearing. We were all born with faults. We were born with fissures (splits and cracks in our foundation), which are passed down from generation to generation. It is only a matter of time before the faults erupt under the three types of pressure.

Tension
The first pressure is tension. Tension pulls a person apart forcing opposite sides away from each other. In this context, it is the pressure of being torn between right and wrong. This is directly related to sinful behavior and our flesh. Galatians 5:17 says: *"For we naturally love to do evil things that are just the opposite from the things that the Holy Spirit tells us to do; and the good things we want to do when the Spirit has his way with us are just the opposite of our natural desires. These two forces within us are constantly fighting each other to win control over us, and our wishes are never free from their pressures."* (New Living Bible)

We can know what we are supposed to do, but we have a craving for the forbidden pulling us. When you think of this as tension in a person's heart, it adjusts our view about what a fault is.

The tension will identify the fault; the place in us that is weak or broken. This is the place most likely to cave in under this kind of pressure. That is why sin is not only a behavior, but it is a condition of the heart. The earthquake (behavior) is the manifestation of a deeper issue. The deeper issue is that we were born fractured. We were born fragile and broken. The sinful expression simply indicates that another earthquake has occurred inside of us. You could easily sum up tension in these three ways: Lust of the flesh, Lust of the eye, and the Pride of life (which keeps our lust and pain in darkness and secrecy).

Compression

The second pressure is compression. Compression is the squeezing of opposites sides against each other. Sometimes the stress on our lives is not necessarily direct enticements to sinful behavior, but it is our response to life itself. Most of us feel squeezed in by at least three categories of life's everyday issues. They are the pressures of:

1.) Daily Responsibility
2.) Internal Expectations
3.) Societal Images

The pressures of everyday life have literally caused mental and emotional breakdowns in many people. Usually at the top of the list are the pressures of going to work every day, dealing with people and paying bills.

When you hate your job and work only because you have bills to pay, that leads to more intense compression. The demands of rent, utilities, loans, insurance, food and clothing have many of us under so much pressure that we cannot sleep.

Often walking hand in hand with daily responsibility is the expectations you have on yourself. Most people live with a mental timeline of where they want to be by the time they reach a certain age.

We have encountered too many over-driven people. Society calls it self-motivated, but when you have your life on an unrealistic timeline, you cause yourself untold, needless heartache and pain. Today's mass media has done a great job in promoting youthfulness. They have taken the honor out of maturity and the things that are worth waiting for.

Thousands are in the rat race trying to beat the societal deadlines to acquire success NOW. It is a serious compression that is squeezing you until you have an internal earthquake.

Shearing

The third pressure that we live with is shearing. Shearing is: violent glancing blows that slice off parts of a rock, surface or foundation.

Many of us are not only broken because of the tension of sin and the compressions of life, but we have been seriously damaged due to violent encounters in life (shearing).

Shearing is direct conflict and confrontation. The natural results of shearing are that parts and pieces of our heart have been torn off. There is damage, defacing and destruction.

For many who are reading this book, it wasn't until marriage that much of the damage of shearing began to surface in your life. You came to realize the specific parts and places that had been sheared.

Those who grew up under domination, manipulation, intimidation, abuse (emotional, verbal, physical, or sexual), violence, poverty, divorce, desertion, or separation, were reluctantly forced to see how shearing affected their outlook on life. This affects their ability and willingness to go through life's necessary transitions and changes.

Salt of the Earth

Dr. Lynn Lucas, who pastors the Fountainhead Church in Elwood (E. Northport), New York, once shared with our congregation the interesting fact that in places where there are high concentrations of salt, there are few, if any earthquakes. This is because, under pressure, salt liquefies and filters into cracks and crevices and holds the broken places together, thus preventing violent earthquakes.

Dr. Lucas taught us that, in the Bible, salt represents a preserving element as well as a covenant commitment. We believe that your recovery is going to involve some covenantal relationships and life preserving steps to see you through the process of healing and restoration from the damage of tension, compression and shearing. Although we didn't know it at the time, that's what happened when we made our PACT.

Salt (covenant and healing) was applied in one another's faults. That's what God is seeking to bring to you and your relationships. If you are separated or divorced, that's what God was seeking to do for you back when you were together, but He can still do it for you today.

Now, it's time to decide how the salt will be applied in your life from this day forward. Just don't try to preserve yourself while avoiding close relationships because of your pain. You run the risk of being isolated and alone with the tremors that are warning you of more impending quakes.

If you're married, pass the salt! Talk about your broken places. Trust your spouse with this new level of covenant. We also encourage you to get involved in a church or its home Bible study and fellowships: married, unmarried, single parents or life after divorce ministries, where you can establish healthy and preserving elements, along with covenant bonding that will help you deal with tension, compression and shearing pressures.

We strongly recommend the book, "No Longer a Victim," co-authored by Dr. Lynn Lucas and Burton Stokes. It is a great source of guidance and healing for you in this time of your life.

If you're thinking about marriage, thinking about a divorce, or trying to figure out why you got married in the first place, this season of your life can be one of healing and repairs instead of perpetual pain and endless hurting. Please don't remain alone and isolated. We know there is great risk in stepping outside the safety zone of your own thoughts, experiences and secrets, but it is worth the risk. Yes, there will be moments of pain, but you can have a life of healing.

Rehabbing Your Heart
We think of it like this: If you severely sprain or break your ankle, there will be tremendous pain as a physician examines you and does whatever is necessary to set it and wrap it. There will be days of pain that follow as you work to rehabilitate the injury, but because you are moving in the right direction, towards healing, you endure the pain and keep working with the injured area.

Eventually you will see and feel the healing. We believe it is the same where you have experienced emotional, psychological and spiritual injuries.

Our PACT launched us on a journey that brought healing to one another. It was the fulfillment of the Word of God. We confessed our faults (broken places) to one another and healing came into our hearts, our minds, our souls and our bodies.

We're not any more special than anybody else. We're just a couple of inner city kids who fell in love, messed up a lot along the way, and made a promise. We don't know what God's strategy will be for you, but HE has one and you can live it.

From Slavery to Promise
In 1 Corinthians 10:1-15, the Apostle Paul describes the journey of the Hebrew people from Egypt to the Land of Promise. We have taught our church family that this passage depicts the journey of Believers who are coming out of slavery to sin, going through a wilderness transition, and moving into God's purpose for their lives.

Paul reminded everyone that along the way, there were several trials that they encountered and in each trial there was a specific temptation that came with it. They had no water, no food, and no protection from the elements or wild animals. At one point, the leader disappeared for over a month. When they finally reached their goal, people who were bigger and stronger occupied the land. So they saw no way to actually be able to take possession of it.

Why would God allow them to go through such a difficult season? We believe it was so that He could change them and prepare them for their ultimate purpose. They had been slaves for over 400 years, so they had a slavery mentality. They needed a transition period. Even though they had been taken out of slavery, they had to get slavery out of them. Even though they had been taken out of poverty, they had to get poverty out of them. Even though they had been taken out of the Egyptian culture, they had to get that culture taken out of them.

God allowed them to come to situations where there was no water so they would learn to look to Him. He let them run out of food, so they would learn to be fed by Him. He called the leader away for a long time, so they would learn to look to Him. He let them see the gigantic people in the promise land, so they would learn to compare the giants to Him, and not compare themselves to the giants.

Perhaps God is taking you through this kind of transition. You may be in the midst of a wilderness journey right now. Please heed the warnings from Paul in 1 Corinthians 10. He told them that even though there would be temptation to become idolaters, commit sexual immorality, tempt Christ and complain, that no temptation would be more than what they could bear because God would provide a way of escape.

The way of escape is not to get out of the wilderness or the trial, but according to James 1, *Blessed is the man who endures temptation*. He goes on to say, *Let no one say when he is tempted, "I am tempted by God"; for God cannot be tempted by evil, nor does He Himself tempt anyone. But each one is tempted when he is drawn away by his own desires and enticed*.

God allows the trials in your wilderness journey so you can uncover those hidden desires that are going to prevent you from successfully walking out your purpose. He is taking you through the wilderness to prepare you for your land of promise. He's getting that old slavery mentality out of you.

The way of escape from the temptation is found by seeking the wisdom of God for what you are going through. Wisdom provides vital answers for those questions that come with trials. What is God's perspective on your situation? What is He accomplishing through you? What is He revealing about Himself?

Some of our heroes include family members and close friends who have triumphed over painful separations and divorces.

95

Today, many of you are dynamic speakers and powerful worshippers who flow in prophetic, encouraging ministry. Some are recording artists, youth ministry leaders, and working in a myriad of professions. Behind the success, you are single parents who went through the devastation of a divorce.

It took many years to recover, but the point is that you did. God took you through the wilderness and into His purpose. He took you out of divorce and then took divorce out of you, so that you could become a minister of His healing.

We know you thought this book was only about marriage, but we tricked you didn't we? This book is also about your decision to commit your heart and life to God so completely that HE can use YOU to bring healing into the lives of those who live and work with you every day.

Knowing that HE was going to allow His people to go into seventy years of captivity, God made them a promise. It was: *For I know the thoughts that I think toward you, says the LORD, thoughts of peace and not of evil, to give you a future and a hope.* (Jeremiah 29: 11, NKJV)

Before you were taken captive, God already had this promise in place for you. Now is the time for you to believe it, receive it, and step into it. You already have the hope. Your future begins today.

God's prescription for trust elevated our marriage. We encourage you to give serious consideration to this part of the PACT as well.

If you are reading this book with your spouse or fiancée, just turn to them right now and speak these words. If you are unmarried speak them to God:

"I promise to trust you with truth and transparency.
I promise to trust you with my faults and broken places. I promise to trust you."

Climate Change

Weather patterns have been pretty bizarre throughout the world the past few years. From floods in Australia to frost in Florida, this has been very strange. Some feel that we may be in the midst of a global climate change.

The weather has been sort of like our marriages and relationships. With all the strange outbreaks and abnormal temperatures, the most difficult aspect is the feeling that there's nothing we can do about it except wait it out and see what happens next.

Thankfully, we were always able to turn back to our PACT when we experienced strange weather patterns in our marriage. Sudden and unexpected storms can hit a marriage in many forms. Financial setbacks, in-laws, parental challenges, and work schedules can provide a constant stream of thunderstorms and tornadoes, but the most devastating damage is often done by the overall climate change in the relationship itself.

Scientifically speaking, climate changes are the result of a sustained atmospheric change. The atmosphere in your heart affects the atmosphere in your home. When it becomes cold, cynical, critical, negative and fearful inside your heart, it becomes cold, cynical, critical, negative and fearful in your home. After a while, it's cold for so long that it's not just a season of winter, but it becomes a cold climate all year long, with only brief periods of sunshine or warmth.

When we think back over the years of our marriage, we are so thankful that the Lord gave us the precepts and prescriptions of the PACT. They helped us establish a warm and gentle climate that occasionally experienced seasons of storms and cold, instead of a cold and stormy climate that only sees sunshine for a couple days or weeks per year.

The secret to establishing a loving climate was to yield our hearts to God the Father, and by constantly surrendering our wills to the Holy Spirit. That's what helped us to continue to be honest with ourselves, so that we could be transparent with one another.

This level of vulnerability caused us to recognize when love and respect were being exchanged and given to one another. As I loved my wife, she respected me. As she respected me, I loved her. Since we had been accountable and open, we were able to recognize when something was being said or done through love and when something was being said or done out of respect. Without that recognition, we would have overlooked or dismissed the words and deeds that were communicating our love and respect for one another.

The PACT showed us how to resist the temptation to only focus on what the other person should be doing for me. This kind of focus is what causes a cold, cynical, critical, negative and fearful marriage. God reset our mindset to begin serving, helping and ministering to one another.

You may have been thinking that when it comes to your marriage and relationships that bad luck has been following you. You may feel that some demon is hovering over your life. You may be wondering why you seem to attract the wrong kind of people.

When we browse through various Facebook pages of friends and friends of friends, we have observed a disturbing amount of negative postings surrounding relationship issues. People will post that they are in a relationship and then two months later, the status changes to complicated. A few days after that, they're back to single again.

We'd like to offer this one final word of advice. Instead of looking for happiness and fulfillment in another person, start working on your own inner healing. If you're not happy, begin with you; because if you don't properly love you, no one else can make you happy, either.

When people enter into your life, there might be some chilly blast coming from you. You may think you're being sweet, polite, cordial, kind and loving, but what they FEEL coming from you is very different from what you project.

Perhaps you are asking: Shouldn't I be able to expect something different if I enter a relationship with a Christian

Believers? Let's look at it this way. They're just people, like you, who are in a process, just like you. If you go into a relationship expecting them to be the mature one whose supposed to only help you through your process, then you don't understand the true depths of human relationships or the damage that is still within most of us. You will expect them to forgive all your flaws, while you mercilessly condemn theirs. That's the 'vibe' others may be picking up from you and that's why the negative cycle continues. Your climate may be too cold.

There is nothing like waking up in the morning and asking the Lord, *How can I minister Your love to my spouse, friends, or family today?* We are living witnesses that this is not a fantasy. This became our reality. Even when we went through times where we got way off track and missed one another by miles in our communication, because our climate was one of warmth, love, unconditional acceptance, and total commitment to what is best for the other person, the cold days and stormy nights could not and did not last long. We were able to weather tornadoes, floods and earthquakes.

Determine, now that you want that kind of relationship. If whether you are married, divorced, separated, or single and not even looking, begin to change the atmosphere in your own heart. Get away from being cold, cynical, critical, negative and fearful. Whatever you sustain inside of you, that atmosphere, over time, will become the CLIMATE of your HEART.

If you make this change and establish a climate of warmth, your entire perspective on life will enlarge. The best part is that your children, nieces and nephews will see real love modeled in front of them every day. When the time comes for them to venture out into the world; when they are seeking their purpose in life and their long-term relationships, they will have a standard established in their hearts of what Godly friends, connections and marriage are supposed to be. They can move forward and establish a promise of accountability, commitment and trust for their homes and families.

Acknowledgements

All Glory to Father God, His Son and our savior Jesus Christ, and the Holy Spirit who teaches and guides us daily.

Our sons: Christopher Michael, Jonathan Mark and David Matthew Green

Bishop Raphael and Pastor Brenda Green
Metro Christian Worship Center/ Urban Pastors and Leaders Alliance
St. Louis, Missouri

James and La-Verna Fountain
The Alphabets of Life - Defiant Hope Consulting and Training Company

Pastor Joseph and Gwen Green
Antioch Assembly, Harrisburg, PA

Pastor Dave and Sheri Hess
Christ Community Church, Camp Hill, PA

Pastor Mark and Dr. Dawn Lawrence
Kingdom First Ministries, Chesapeake, VA

Pastor Dave and the late Geraldine Parker
Prime Time Ministry: The Worship Center, Lancaster, PA

Pennsylvania Council of Churches

Hosea and Amethyst Roberson
A.R. Licensed Professional Counseling, St. Louis, MO

John and Kerry Shuey
Kingdom Quest Ministries, Camp Hill, PA

Apostle A.E. and the late Pastor Denise Sullivan
The Victory Outreach Christian Church, Harrisburg, PA

Drs. Clarence and Ja'Ola Walker
Fresh Anointing Christian Center, Upper Darby, PA

Pastor Raleigh and Renee Wingfield
Zion Assembly of Harrisburg, PA

Chrys Yvette, Chrys Yvette Productions
Serenity Arts and Entertainment

Bibliography and References

(All information is accessible via various web search engines)

Achieving Marriage Oneness - Dr. Dennis Rainey
Family Life Today

Blue Letter Bible.org (Encyclopedias and Dictionaries)

Breaking Free to Your Destiny – John and Kerry Shuey
Kingdom Quest Ministries

Caring for People God's Way - Dr. Tim Clinton
American Association of Christian Counselors

Circle of Contentment - Drs. Clarence and Ja'Ola Walker
Clarence Walker Ministries

Five Love Languages – Dr. Gary Chapman
Marriage and Family Life

Gateway Searchable Online Bible

Love and Respect - Dr. Emerson & Sarah Eggerichs
Love and Respect Ministries

No Longer a Victim - Burton Stokes and Dr. Lynn Lucas

Teaching Series: Atmospheres, Climates, Dimensions
Bishop Tudor Bismark, Tudor Bismark Ministries

Teaching Video Message: Pruning
Chuck Mingo, Crossroads Church, Cincinnati, Oho

Vine's Expository Online Dictionary of New Testament Words

What NOW (Chapter 9) – Christopher G. Green
Fruitful Life Network of Ministries, Inc.

About the Authors

Chris and Carol Green are a husband and wife team that was sent to south central Pennsylvania to help rebuild, restore and renew hearts and homes. They are certified master life coaches, urban marriage and family advisers, leadership and community outreach consultants, and ordained ministers.

They served in local church pastoral leadership in St. Louis, MO and Harrisburg, PA for a combined 27 years, before they launched a three-part initiative that would synergies their professional expertise with their ministry experience in a network of community services and leadership training.

Their community-supporting initiatives have included hosting monthly workshops in a state-funded unemployment center, on-call life coaching support for a women's transitional housing shelter, consultation and training for local outreach organizations, collaborating with various community outreach efforts, and maintaining an itinerant schedule of local and national speaking engagements and opportunities.

For their community service, they received a United Way 2017 Volunteer of the Year Nomination. They have also received Urban Leadership Awards (2016) and Community Ambassador Awards (2015) from iChange Nations™ and were appointed Goodwill Ambassadors of World Peace, as part of an interfaith peace-building initiative to the United Nations, by Golden Rule International.

Chris Green is a social media veteran and an award-winning producer of a local cable television broadcast (1999). Together, they have been international columnists/writers with a Global Journalism Award-winning social media news team, the authors of several inspirational life-building books, and the creators of numerous blogs and eNewsletters. They are also accomplished songwriters, having penned and produced over 150 songs since 1992.

Their travels have taken them from coast to coast in the United States, to Hawaii, the Bahamas, Trinidad, the United Kingdom, and West Africa.

They have been married since January 3, 1981 and have three adult sons, two daughters-in-law, one granddaughter, and a host of people throughout the world who call them 'mom and dad'.

Access more insight and inspiration from Chris and Carol Green through their internet outreach.

The PACT *(Marriage and Family Enrichment and Resiliency)*
www.fruitful-life.net/wemadeapact

Fight 4 Your Family
https://vimeo.com/channels/fight4yourfamilyseries

Fruitful Living *(Online Class)*
https://vimeo.com/channels/fruitfullivingclassroom

iHave Value (Awaken the Dream Within)
https://vimeo.com/channels/unlockingdreamnuggets

Meant To Be *(Love Songs by Chris and Carol Green)*
www.fruitful-life.net/LoveSongs

Fruitful Life Network, Inc.

www.fruitful-life.net

Made in the USA
Columbia, SC
20 February 2018